Let the Nations Rejoice! An Invitation to Dance

Let the nations rejoice and sing for joy: for thou wilt judge the peoples equitably; and the nations upon earth, thou wilt guide them. Selah.

Psalms 67:4 (Darby Bible Translation)

Let the heavens be glad, and the earth rejoice! Tell all the nations, "The LORD reigns!"
I Chronicles 16:31 (New Living Translation)

Dr. Pamela Hardy

Copyright © 2011
Let the Nations Rejoice! An Invitation to Dance
Dr. Pamela Hardy
www.drpamelahardy.org

Printed in the United States of America

Catalogued in the Library of Congress – Publication Department

ISBN –978-0-9839248-3-8

Editorial Assistance
Jabez Books Writers' Agency
(A Division of Clark's Consultant Group)
www.clarksconsultantgroup.com

Unless otherwise stated, scriptural quotations are taken from the New King James Version of the Bible.

LET THE NATIONS

REJOICE!

Dr. Pamela Hardy

Dedication

- I dedicate this book to my Lord and Savior, Jesus Christ. Thank you, Lord, for trusting me to send me to the nations.
- To my parents, Jesse and Ernestine Scott. I am only here because of their love and sacrifice. They are the best parents in the world.
- To my husband, Chris Hardy, whose unwavering love and support keeps me filled with joy each day.
- To Valencia and Nicole, thank you for taking care of the family business at home each time I go away on God's business.
- To Chuck Pierce - your Godly example of leadership touches my life more than words can say.

A Word to Dancers

"The Spirit of the Lord God is upon me, because the Lord has anointed me…" (Isaiah 61:1). Dancers, we must go to the next level! It's time for us to grow up in our gifts and callings. It's time for us to realize that we are not just dancers; we are ministers of the Gospel of Jesus Christ. We must spend time in the council room of Heaven until His voice is heard. It is then and only then can we be released to dance His dances – dances that are from Heaven, His throne, and His heart. We need dances that will set the captives free. Dances that will bind up the broken hearted and proclaim liberty to the captives.

Dancers, it is time for us to realize the responsibility we have been given. We must recognize it is not the time to be idle or to be caught up in the cares of this world. Dancer, this is not a time to be out of place! Nor is it time to hold on to secret sins. **It is time for us to long for Him, to seek Him with all of our hearts.** Cry out for a release of His presence, and then rise up and go forth to "dance" His purposes.

There is a prophetic generation in the womb of the church – people who will hear from Heaven and declare it in the earth. As dancers, we are to be prophetic demonstrations of what our Heavenly Father is saying and doing. We must be those who also know the purposes of God for our generation – those who know the times and seasons and have knowledge of what to do. We must be those who will leave a legacy to the next generation.

This is the time when God's favor is upon us. This is the time when God is visiting His people. He is putting us in place for His purposes, preparing and equipping us. This is the time that God is moving in our midst like never before. This is the time when God is bringing His promises to pass. In some, God is planting seeds. In others, He is placing His vision for their lives. In many, He is releasing them into DESTINY – His purposes for their lives. Let us pray for strength to bring forth, strength to walk in the call.

The time for the new release of God's anointing is NOW! For those who are hidden in Him -- new dances -- dances that will bring the fire of His Spirit. God is changing things in His house, marking us for His purposes. New winds are blowing in God's Kingdom. Believe, receive...Your time is now!

STAY FOCUSED.

A Challenge to ARISE and WAKE UP!

We are living in very strategic and prophetic times. Daniel 11:32 states, "...but the people that do know their God shall be strong, and do great exploits." God is raising up an anointed army of believers. The Lord is releasing us to be offensive by raising up a praying church that operates in the prophetic anointing with signs and wonders; healing and deliverance. With this in mind, we must endeavor each day to receive a fresh impartation of the Holy Spirit that we might rise up to become prophetically gifted people with a heart after God alone.

These end-times require a radical people with radical worship, and a radical love for God. Let those arise who are willing to let go of the past, let go of religion, let go of tradition to press into their God ordained purpose. Each of us must determine to be a prophetic people willing to learn the secrets of the secret place.

These end-times are calling for people with an apostolic mandate from God to go forth into the entire world to preach the Gospel. This end-time harvest will be won by worshipping warriors, carrying the fire of God, sold out to the cause of Christ.

To be a part of the Reformation Movement of the church, we must be those who see the need for reform and change, then cry out to God--He alone can bring forth His bride. God is trying to shift us into a new place. Truly, the latter day church will be greater than the former. So ARISE and WAKE UP CHURCH! Lay aside the sin and weight, which does so easily beset us and run with patience the race that is set before us (Hebrews

12:1). Receive the anointing from *"On High"* that will propel you into destiny and allow you to dance the dances for the entire world to see.

The nations are crying out for dances of victory that will set the captives free!

Table of Contents

A Word to Dancers

Dancers from Mexico

Dancers from Fiji

Dancers from Puerto Rico

Chapter One

IN THE BEGINNING
Call to the Nations

n the beginning, there was first position and 5, 6, 7, 8! As far back as I can remember I took dance lessons. I grew up in a very small town in Tennessee, which had very limited cultural resources. But despite its cultural limitations, my mother was still able to locate a school of dance to enroll me. The truth is I do not remember very much. I am not sure how many people remember things that happened when they were three years old. But that is when I first stepped my feet into a dance studio, I imagine it might have gone something like this:

What an exciting day! As I wake this morning (I imagine that in my three year old mind) the sun is shining brighter than ever! It is going to be an exciting day! My first day at dance class! Just imagine! ME! Leaping and dancing across the stage in a beautiful costume, twirling and turning! I am so excited!

I arrived at dance class. The teacher enters the room, dress in a black leotard, pink tights, pink shoes, and a black ballet skirt. She introduces herself. "Hello. My name is Joy White. I will be your ballet teacher. What is your name?" We each introduce ourselves one at a time – Maria, Yolanda, Catherine, Connie, Pamela, etc. I am sure I was not doing much at that time since I was only three! Whether my mother realized it or not, God was beginning to shape my destiny.

Our teacher then began to tell us that there are five positions in ballet and she showed us each position. "First position," she began, "starts with your feet together. Now keep your heels together and lift your toes and turn your toes outward. Make sure your turn out comes from your hip sockets." She demonstrated for us – the movements seemed easy enough to me. I was on my way to becoming a dancer!

Little did I know that I would have many days of hard work and going back over the correct way **to stand in first position over and over and over again! Whew!**

I spent many days in dance studios as I was growing up in Tennessee. But when I was seven years old, we moved to Kansas City, Missouri. My mother was determined to keep me in dance class, so the search for the "best" studio in our area was underway. We were directed to the Smith Sisters Dance Studio. I remember walking in and being instructed on how to once again, stand in first position!

So every Tuesday, Friday and Saturday, I went to dance class -- ballet, tap and jazz. The Smith Sisters, Kay and YiYi, were like an extra set of mothers! Whenever I did not want to do my bar work or work extra hard on a tap combination, they told my mother! So I decided to work hard all the time.

As it turned out, my grade school years, as well as my high school years were spent in the Smith Sisters Dance Studio. One of the things I loved most about Kay and YiYi was that they exposed their students to many new things and many opportunities to dance in the city. It did not matter to them that we were an African American dance studio. They wanted us to be the best and if there was an audition coming up, they prepared us for it and took us to it.

Kansas City has an outdoor theater named Starlight Theater. In the summer, they would bring in top quality shows and hire local children to be in them. I remember auditioning for such musicals as **Bye Bye Birdie** and **Music Man**. I was always chosen to be a part of the musicals. It was fun and they actually paid us! I danced at Starlight Theater every summer from ages 11-14.

We also auditioned for the professional baseball and football teams! I was also chosen to be a part of their dance teams. I danced for the Kansas City Royals baseball team and the Kansas City Chiefs football team. Growing up in Kansas City was fun. It afforded us opportunities we might not have had growing up in a small town.

Once during the spring, our high school history class went on a field trip to England, Germany, Switzerland and Italy. That was my first introduction to international travel. I am sure that my parents had no idea God would call me to travel to the nations with Him. But God knew.

Although I grew up in the church, I did not know the Lord. I am so glad that He knows us long before we know Him! I had no idea He was guiding my steps all the way and teaching me things I would need once I came to know Him.

When I graduated from high school, I attended Tennessee State University, my father's alma mater. In fact, many of my family members graduated from TSU! With all the wonderful things I was learning about dance, it made perfect sense that I would go to school to become a nurse (smile)! I should have known that nursing was not for me, but I learned some valuable principles that would stay with me forever in life.

My college days were fun. I danced as a majorette for our football team, pledged a sorority and won a beauty contest! At the urging of a friend, I accompanied her in signing up for the Miss Black Expo pageant. I won and was given the title Miss Black Expo and Miss Black Nashville. I then competed in the Miss Black Tennessee pageant. I won again! I then competed and placed as a finalist in the Miss Black American pageant. I graduated with a degree in nursing. Those were exciting days.

I then moved to Dallas, Texas and worked as a registered nurse for a short period of time. As I was learning to care for others, I found myself dancing in the halls of the hospitals! I began to dance with a well known dance company that traveled and performed throughout the state of Texas. The Director of the company also taught dance at Southern Methodist University. One day he was sick and asked me to go and teach his class at the University. With much fear and trembling, I went and met the Dean of the Dance Department. By the end of the class, I was offered a full scholarship to SMU along with a job to teach dance in the evenings to the non-credit students! My life was beginning to go in a direction that was new and exciting!

Dallas also had (and still has) summer theater, The Dallas Summer Musicals. They would bring in Broadway and National Touring companies and hire local talent to be a part of the shows. One of my friends in the dance company asked me to go with her to audition for the summer musicals. I do not think I would have gone to the audition on my own, and as it turned out, I was chosen for the show, she was not. I am sure that neither of us had any idea how that audition would change my life.

After a long, but fun audition, I was chosen to dance and sing in the chorus of **Hello, Dolly!,** with Carol Channing. The show was going on two national tours -- six months each. We went to city after city after city. The show played eight times each week, Tuesday through Sunday, with two shows on Wednesdays and two on Saturday. Monday was our travel day. The pay was very good and I was having fun doing what I loved most. Little did I know that years later God would take me back to some of those same stages to dance for Him.

The cast members of **Hello, Dolly!** encouraged me to audition to be the understudy for one of the principle roles. I got the part! Our show played at the Dorothy Chandler Pavilion in Los Angeles. On opening night, the young lady I was understudying got an urgent phone call from home. She had a family emergency and had to go home right away. That meant she would miss opening night. And that meant that I was to go on in her place! Immediately, I began to panic. It is one thing to practice with the other actors and another thing to speak lines, sing and dance in front of a lot of people -- on opening night! That means newspaper critics were there and would be watching my every move. Thank God I remembered my lines. I was used to dancing in the chorus and honestly, I was quite happy in that role. Things went well, but I was glad when the principal performer returned.

And even though, I performed in tours, I somehow still managed to finish graduate school with a Master of Fine Arts Degree in Dance from SMU. Through the Dallas Summer Musicals, I was also chosen to dance in the regional touring productions of **Little Me** with Donald O'Connor and Eve Arden and **Annie Get Your Gun** with Florence Henderson.

Now, with school behind me and my union card in my pocket, I went to New York City. It had always been my dream to dance on Broadway. Dancing on Broadway had become my goal. I had a friend who once danced on Broadway, and I thought, "If she could do it, I could do it!"

I auditioned for only a couple of shows and after being in New York for four months, I got my first call. I was chosen to dance in the chorus of an Off Broadway show called Golden Boy. It was while dancing in Golden Boy that I got THE CALL!

A few weeks earlier I had gone to audition for the Broadway show **42nd Street**! Little did I know that the same casting director from The Dallas Summer Musicals was also in New York! I still did not know the Lord, but God had given me favor with her and she wanted me to be in her show once again. When the call came, it was to be a part of the California Company of 42nd Street. But before the day was over, one of the cast members had turned in her two week notice and there was an opening in the Broadway Company!

I remember the excitement of my first night of dancing on Broadway. The lights – the people – the costume changes!

I had achieved my dream of dancing on Broadway. There is no place like New York City! I loved riding the bus to and from the theatre just to take in the sites. One day while riding home, I began to feel empty inside. I remember thinking that there must be more to life than eating, sleeping and going to work. Dance had become work.

The hit show **Dreamgirls** was also on Broadway at the time. I had become friends with some of the cast members. They told me about a church that they attended and they invited me to join them.

Although I grew up in the church, I did not grow up with a true knowledge of God. In the church where I grew up in, all I knew to do was sleep for the hour we were there! But I have discovered that God knows us long before we know Him, and His word does not return void. My Father and Mother knew enough to bring me up in the admonition of the Lord. I was soon to find out that His Word was true. As Proverbs 22:6 says, "Train up a child in the way he should go and when he is old, he will not depart from it."

As I walked into the church, I saw people who were filled with joy. They seemed to be alive with hope. The church was home to many people who were in the arts – professional singers, dancers, musicians, song writers, actors, etc.

Pastor Maria preached a sermon that made me ask, "Who told her about me? How did she know all those things about me?" I answered the call when she asked, "Who wants to give their heart to Jesus Christ today?" I ran to the front with tears in my eyes, not even sure why I was crying, just feeling as if life was suddenly absolutely, incredibly wonderful! Thus, began my incredible journey with Christ.

I will always thank God for Pastor Maria. She taught us to love the Lord, to love His Word and to worship Him. Because many in the church were from a performance background, she taught us the difference in *performance and worship*. I remember experiencing some of the most anointed times of worship there. The release of God's anointing on the gifts He had given to those in the congregation proved to be a powerful and prophetic manifestation of God's Spirit **in** the earth. It was truly an awesome, life changing experience. It was there that God called me to the ministry of dance and began to show me the destiny He had for me.

Back in the dance studio, things seemed different now. I still went to ballet class, but now I was dancing with a new partner and I was dancing for a different reason. First position was now different. I still had to put my heels together and turn out properly, but my heart was turned upward. What came to mind was the scripture in Romans 12:1, "I beseech the brethren, by the mercies of God, that you present your bodies a living sacrifice, holy and acceptable to God which is your reasonable worship. And be not conformed to this world, but be ye transformed by the renewing of your mind, that you might prove what is that good, and acceptable, and perfect will of God."

My first position was no longer with my heels together, turned out from the hip sockets. My first position was an **attitude of worship**. God touching me and me touching God in response, with my heart turned upward toward my Father.

Not only did my focus in the studio change, my priorities changed. I learned the importance of beginning each day with God. He became the first position of my heart each day. I quieted my heart before Him. I did not answer the telephone. I turned off the television. I sat alone with God and prepared a place for Him.

I Chronicles 15:1-2 says, "David prepared a place for the ark of God and pitched a tent for it. Then David said, no one may carry the ark of God but the Levites, for the Lord has chosen them to carry the ark of God and to minister before Him forever." I learned that we must take time daily to be a prepared place for the ark, the presence of God, to reside. The world certainly cannot carry His presence. He has chosen us to carry His presence to the world. Psalm 22:3 indicates that as we worship God, He inhabits our praises. We become a dwelling place for the Spirit of God and we can then take His light into the world to overcome any darkness.

One of the things I loved about the church in New York is that we would take a church trip each year. One year we went to Hawaii. We toured the island, ate local food, learned a bit of the language and ministered the Word through dance, song and drama. One of my favorite memories is when we were sitting under a tree, learning how to sing a Hawaiian song based on John 14:6, that Jesus was the way, the truth and the life. I can still remember that song!

We did outreach with some of the local churches and we also had some time to relax and fellowship with each other and with the Lord.

One morning while having my morning time with the Lord, I was sitting on the balcony of my hotel room looking out over the ocean. As I was caught up in His presence, the Lord began to speak to me. He said, **"I am going to take you all over the world to dance for me."** My reply was "Yes, Lord. Your will be done."

I was shocked to hear those words! I had no idea what that meant! In fact, I am still learning what this meant. This one thing I do know, though: He has called the nations to rejoice and He has called me to be a part of His wonderful plan.

Be sure to begin your first position with a heart that is ready to receive from Him. John 10:27 says, "My sheep hear my voice, and I know them, and they follow me." Know that His thoughts toward you are good, not evil, to give you hope and a future, Jeremiah 29:11.

Chapter Two

CALL TO THE NATIONS

This church trip was heavenly.

A few years later after receiving Christ into my life, I received a brochure announcing an upcoming worship and dance conference hosted by Mikhael Murnane and Jerusalem Worship Dance. The conference was in Maryland and I lived in Illinois, but I knew that some way, somehow, I was supposed to be there. I drove to the conference and when I arrived and began to experience the worship, I knew that I had just entered heaven on earth.

Worship was led by Paul Wilbur. The instructors were Valerie Henry, Yvonne Peters and Mikhael. Although I wondered why I had not been exposed to this level of worship before, I was elated that my appointed time to enter into a new season had come. The joy that I experienced there was overwhelming! I learned so much from each instructor. In one of the classes taught by Yvonne Peters, she prophesied to me saying, **"God has called you to the nations."** I wondered what that meant! Then I remembered the words God had spoken to me on that balcony in Hawaii several years earlier and my answer was still, "Yes, Lord. Your will be done."

When I met Valerie Henry for the first time, I had no idea she was the choreographer for the Feast of Tabernacles held each year in Israel. I only knew that to see Valerie dance before the Lord was to experience a beauty and a grace that can only come from heaven. I said to myself, "God wanted a dancer, so He created Valerie." After getting to know her, I was right. Her humility and genuine heart reflect the light of the Lord in a beautiful way. Yvonne served as Valerie's assistant at the Feast in Israel. Today, she has become my mentor and trusted friend. Her life has taught me the importance of having a pure heart before God. Little did I know that not only would I be invited to be one of the teachers on staff with Mikhael, Valerie and Yvonne, but I was invited to be a member of the Tabernacle Dance Company at the Feast of Tabernacles held each year in Israel. As all of this was unfolding in my life, God reminded me about a prophecy I received years ago, that He would call me to dance at the Feast in Israel. Now I was seeing His word fulfilled in my life.

Israel! My first international ministry trip – it was an experience that could have only come from the heart of God. We stayed there for three weeks, rehearsing everyday in a studio that overlooked the Mount of Olives. Each day the team shared in Bible study, dance technique and learning choreography for the seven day Feast of Tabernacles that was to follow.

The Feast is sponsored by the International Christian Embassy Jerusalem. People come from around the world to bless Israel and to pray for the peace of Jerusalem. Zechariah 14:16 tells us that "the nations...shall come up from year to year to worship the King, the Lord of hosts, and to keep the Feast of Tabernacles." The Feast was a time of unity and joy. Many celebrations would take place during the Feast. As I saw hundreds of God's people from over 100 countries rejoicing around the throne of God, I saw the Word of God come alive like never before. It was an incredible experience. And as a dancer, I encourage you to learn more about this organization. Log onto this website: www.icej.org and be blessed.

This was such a defining moment in my life. I knew this was that. This is what God had ordained for me in life. He had called me to the nations.

Several years later, I had a dream. It was a dream that I was in Jerusalem, in a beautiful green field. There was an urgency in my spirit and I was telling everyone: **"Jesus is coming soon! Jesus is coming soon!"** I kept saying these words over and over. Suddenly, I heard a trumpet blast and I looked up! The heavens were about to open! Then I woke up. Not sure of all what God was saying through this dream, but I know for a surety, the return of the Lord is near. Therefore, we must be about our Father's business. God has placed on the heart of my husband Christopher, and I, to take teams to the nations on what we call a prayer tour. We go to the land to bless Israel and pray for the peace of Jerusalem. We dance, sing, prophesy, declare and release His Word in the nation of Israel. Perhaps I will be there one day when I hear that trumpet blast that I heard in my dream. Since the day I sat on that hotel balcony in Hawaii, God has allowed me to go with Him to over 25 nations. I am honored that God would use me this way and to touch so many nations. Below is a list of the nations I have ministered in and I pray that it will leave you with a global perspective of God's Kingdom.

Anguilla
Australia
Bahamas
Barbados
Canada
Costa Rica
Curacao
Dominica
Ecuador
England
Fiji
Germany
Israel
Jamaica

Malaysia
Mexico
Netherlands
Nicaragua
Panama
Scotland
South Africa
St. Lucia
St. Maarten
Suriname
Tortola
Trinidad
Turkey
United States and Puerto Rico

It is as if I heard the voice of the Lord say to my heart, **"Whom shall I send and who will go for Us?"** My heart answered, "Here am I! Send me."

Chapter Three

EVANGELIZING THE NATIONS THROUGH DANCE

S tudies show that a greater percentage of people remember what they see more often than what they hear. For that reason, dance can be used as a powerful tool for evangelism. Presenting the messages of God to people through movement can minister to them just as effectively as the preached Word.

Luke 4:18 says:

> The Spirit of the Lord is upon me,
> Because the Lord has anointed me
> To preach good tiding s to the meek
> He has sent ME to heal the brokenhearted,
> To proclaim liberty to the captives
> And the recovery of sight to the blind,
> To set at liberty those who are oppressed;
> To proclaim the acceptable year of the Lord.

This original commission was given to Jesus, and since we, the body of Christ, is an extension of Jesus, then it is our commission, too. As New Testament Christians, we have a mandate to "do the work of an Evangelist." The word *"Evangelist"* is only found in the New Testament. It means to preach the gospel, to announce good news, to declare good tidings. We are not just dancers, we are ministers of the Gospel and we need to begin to see ourselves as ministers of God's Word through dance. We must order our lifestyle accordingly and approach ministry with that in mind. **We are not performers nor are we entertainers.** Therefore, there must be clarity in what we are presenting.

As New Testament Christians, we have received the power of the Holy Spirit to do the works of Christ in the earth today. We have an apostolic mandate that God gave us in Mark 16:15 that tells us to "Go ye into all the world and preach the gospel." Today, this is an unfinished task and there are several reasons that exist that keep the Gospel from reaching everyone in the world. Some of the most common challenges are: language, political, social and religious barriers. Of the millions of people on the earth, there are still many yet to be reached with the Good News of the Gospel.

John 3:16 is a scripture almost people know, "For God so loved the world that He gave His only begotten son, that whosoever believes in Him will not perish but will have everlasting life."

Acts 15:16 says God will restore the tabernacle of David, the place where worship was first set in order, so that men may seek after the Lord. Our praise and worship are supposed to cause people to want to know Him.

Jesus came to seek and save the lost. Those who are well do not need a physician. The church must grow up and be "well" enough to go out and "compel" them to come into God's house -- God desires that His house be full. This requires us to go beyond ourselves. It also requires us to go beyond the dance itself, and yield our hearts to the Spirit of the Lord, who is the Lord of the dance.

Ask God to give you His heart for the lost. Ask God to increase your vision that you may see from His viewpoint and understand the enormity of the task of the church. It is harvest time. Are you willing to be a laborer in God's field? Will you go? Whether it is to prisons, nursing homes or across the ocean to another country, will you go?

Some of us would not need to go far to reach another people group. America is made up of many different people and many of them are in our very own neighborhoods. We have cultural differences within our own cities, within our local churches.

The church has a tremendous responsibility to take the Gospel to all nations. We have been given the keys of the Kingdom to establish His Kingdom in the hearts of men.

We are *called* to be disciples and to *help* make disciples. **God desires a functioning, alive, indigenous and reproducing church in every people group.** Evangelism has two parts: (1) the actual message; (2) the delivery system that gets the message to its desired target, the hearts of people. We must remember, it is God's message, not our own. We must pray and spend time with God so we will know how to deliver His message to each people group God sends us to. We must ask, "What does God want to say? How does He want to say it?

As a tool of evangelism, dance can be used in many ways with different methods. As we speak God's Word, sing and dance God's Word over people and situations, God will give us the necessary strategies.

To strategize means to manage your resources wisely, i.e. to win a war. Tactics have to do with how the strategy is played out. Therefore, we must be sensitive; yet, bold when incorporating dance, realizing that often times, **people will remember more of what they see than what they hear.**

Movement is a universal language that can transcend any language barrier. Therefore, dance can be a tremendous plus, especially when dealing with people from other countries. In the case of ministering to people from other nations, we must remember not to judge others by our own standards. We cannot judge the culture of others. We must gain a global perspective. We must know our audience, understand cultural differences and dimensions and be willing to adapt to meet the needs of those God sends us to.

Heaven celebrates our cultural differences. Revelation 9:7 says every tribe and tongue will worship God. If He calls us to the nations, we must study the culture, the customs and climate; the food, the economy and the language. Let us consider various cultural dynamics, sociological, ethnological, geographical differences as well as the political history of a nation or people group when called to a nation.

We would minister differently in Israel than we would in Mexico. We would approach ministry from a different perspective if we were called to South Africa or Malaysia. **Seek to redeem the dances of the nations and not to impose our western culture and dances upon them.** Another critical element to this sensitivity is establishing relationships with local churches within each nation.

We are called to be God's messengers to a dark world, whether across the street or across the oceans. If we empty our own dances and make way for His dances to come forth, we can see nations changed.

Study to know the times and the seasons in which we live and to know how, when, why and where you are called to minister God's messages through dance. Ask Him, "Am I called to assemble your people -- to gather them?; to stir them for war?; to call them to repentance?; to comfort them?; or to evangelize them?"

We cannot worry about being rejected or humiliated when we are called to the nations. We just have to obey. Many people have yet to hear or "see" the gospel. Want to go to the nations? Then get a map of the world and begin to pray. Ask God to begin to put a nation or nations in your heart, so that you may be a part of bringing in that harvest.

What can you do? You can support missions and ministries that reach out and/or go to the nations. In addition, you can support local fellowships within nations through financial contributions. Perhaps God will call you to go and live in another nation. Whether short-term or long-term, your life will help to shift and shape a nation. Sometimes we are called to make an impact one life at a time. However you answer the call, tune your ear and your heart to hear the nations calling.

You can stand with them through fasting and prayer. Prayer is an integral part of the global "march" of the church. There is no distance in the Spirit. **You can pray and make a difference as you dance God's Word and earnestly seek God on behalf of others in need.** Ask the Lord to place His love for the nations in your heart.

For those who feel called to go to the nations, be prepared. Get your passport ready and then go ye into all the world and dance the gospel, for the end-time harvest will be won by worshippers consumed with a passion for Jesus Christ.

Dr. Hardy dancing in Jamaica

Dr. Hardy dancing in Suriname

Dr. Hardy dancing in Israel

Chapter Four

LET THE NATIONS SPEAK

Why dance? Dance is an art form that generally refers to movement of the body, including rhythmic movements to music, used as a form of expression, as social interaction or used in a spiritual or performance setting.

Dance may also be regarded as a form of nonverbal communication between humans. Movements made by other animals, i.e., the mating dance of the bee, are considered as dance patterns of behavior. Everything that has life moves. Even motions in ordinarily inanimate objects may also be described as dances, for example, *"the leaves danced in the wind."*

Movement is part of life. The only things that do not move are dead things! So human beings are movers or dancers by nature. Dances can be for celebrations or for an audience. Dances can be for praise or simply movements for exercise or health purposes. But dance apart from worship is simply movement. Dance can communicate ideas, preserve cultural identities, strengthen social bonds, or express the deepest feelings of the heart.

Many nations have folk dances that are indigenous to their culture. International folk dance is a genre of dance wherein selected folk dances from multiple ethnic groups are performed, typically as part of a regular recreational dance (for performances or at other events). The dances are typically considered the products of national or cultural traditions rather than part of an international tradition. Here is a brief look at a few:

Suriname, officially the **Republic of Suriname**, is a country in northern South America.

Suriname is situated between French Guiana to the east and Guyana to the west. The southern border is shared with Brazil and the northern border is the Atlantic coast.

I flew to Suriname after leaving Anguilla. The trips were not scheduled together so consequently, I flew back to Miami before flying to Suriname. Four planes later, I landed in Suriname. I later learned that there was a much quicker route.

The country of Suriname is beautiful and the people are wonderfully open and warm. In Suriname, I received a welcome like never before. I had the opportunity to meet with the wife of the President, be interviewed on television, and be featured in local newspapers. The worship of God through dance was a major event! Front page coverage! GLORY!

Our worship time was truly amazing! Eighty worshippers showed up for the workshop. The presence of the Lord was there to meet us. But before I left, I also had the privilege of ministering at a local church on Sunday. Prior to this event, I had originally met this Pastor in the Bahamas, so he was excited to have me there ministering at his church. Young men were filled with the Holy Spirit and a new level of worship was released into the house.

Later on, the host Pastor and his wife took me on a tour of Paramaribo, the city where I stayed. Paramaribo is the capital and largest city of Suriname, located on banks of the Suriname River. As we crossed the largest bridge in Paramaribo, I saw a telephone. When I inquired about the telephone on the bridge, they told me that many young people had jumped from the bridge and the telephone was put there in hopes that they would make a call before they jumped. Pray for Suriname and prophesy that indeed, God will be with them, and that they will see the victory.

Republic of Suriname

Flag
Coat of arms

Motto: Justice - Duty - Loyalty

Anguilla is a British overseas territory in the Caribbean, one of the most northerly of the Leeward Islands in the Lesser Antilles. The island's capital is The Valley. The total land area of the territory has a population of approximately 13,500. Anguilla was first settled by Amerindian tribes who migrated from South America. The earliest Amerindian artifacts found on Anguilla have been dated to around BC 1300, and the remains of settlements date from 600 AD. English is their official language. Most Anguillans belong to Anglican, Methodist or other Protestant churches.

On my first trip to Anguilla, I flew in to St. Maarten. I was met by Diane Rogers Peters. We took a ferry over to Anguilla. It was a beautiful day to sit up top on the ferry, until we hit large waves and the water from the Caribbean ocean drenched us. It was quite a fun beginning to an adventurous stay in Anguilla.

Anguilla is a small, beautiful Island. The people seemed very eager to learn. I met the lady who was the magistrate of Anguilla. Her burden was for the young men of her Island. Because it is a small Island, many people know each other. She would see young men come through her office who were in trouble with the law, young men she had known since they were young.

The people of Anguilla dance during their festivals. You may see various forms, from Latin to Salsa to Tango to Street dancing. During my second trip to Anguilla, we went beyond the walls of the church to the center of the Valley. An outdoor pavilion became our platform for outreach. We danced, sang worship songs, waved flags and banners unto the Lord. The favor of the Lord was with us as we proclaimed that Jesus Christ is Lord over Anguilla! Many people were drawn there by the Spirit of God. Men gave their hearts to the Lord. One young man in particular, shaved his dreadlocks, made a fresh commitment to the Lord and was in church the next morning. For him, the dreadlocks represented a past he was ready to abandon.

Acts 15:16 tells us that part of the reason for the restoration of the Tabernacle of David is to cause people to seek the Lord. That day, we saw that scripture fulfilled before our eyes. Pray for Anguilla – prophesy that the youth of Anguilla will be touched by the Spirit of the Lord and that the church in Anguilla will arise and shine, so that the glory of the Lord will be seen there.   Pray that God will indeed bless Anguilla.

Anguilla

<u>Flag</u>
<u>Coat of arms</u>

<u>Motto</u>: "Strength and Endurance"

Tortola is the largest and most populated of the British Virgin Islands, a group of islands which form part of the archipelago of the Virgin Islands. Local belief is that the name was originally given to the island by Christopher Columbus, meaning "land of the Turtle Dove". But in actuality, Columbus named the island Santa Ana. The Dutch settled, and dubbed it Ter Tholen, after an island off the west coast of the Netherlands. When the British moved in, they altered the name to its present day form of Tortola. Tortola is also known as "Chocolate City."

Tortola is one of the most beautiful places I have ever seen! One must go there to really understand how truly breathtaking it is. My words cannot begin to describe it. Eagle Lizette George covers EITI on the Island of Tortola.

While sailing through the Islands, I knew that someone had to be called to minister in the BVI. I am so glad it was me! We had workshops during the day and worship services in the evenings. One evening during a worship service, the Spirit of the Lord fell upon the youth. These children ranged from ages 7 to 13. I have rarely seen such true and genuine seeking and searching for the presence of God from young children.

A BVI folk dance troupe and local fungi bands (bands made up of guitar, ukulele, washtub bass, scratch gourd, and triangle that play calypso and folk tunes) perform regularly at local cultural events, and represent the BVI at regional cultural festivals. Steel pan music is very popular. Instruction in classical, jazz, and Caribbean music (such as steel pan and fungi) is offered as part of the school music curriculum. Also, local musical talent is showcased at school concerts, in public performance for tourists, and during the annual Festival commemorating emancipation.

Their motto is "Be Watchful." Pray that the church in the BVI will gain a vision for the lost in their nation and throughout the islands. Pray for the youth of the BVI. Pray and prophesy that God will raise up a mighty generation of kingdom warriors who will not be ashamed of the gospel of Jesus Christ. Pray that they will rise up with a passionate desire for all things holy.

British Virgin Islands

Flag
Coat of arms

Motto: "Be Watchful"

Saint Martin (French: *Saint-Martin*; Dutch: *Sint Maarten*) is an island in the northeast Caribbean, approximately 186 miles east of Puerto Rico. The island is divided roughly 60/40 between France and the Netherlands Antilles. It is the smallest inhabited sea island divided between two nations, a division dating to 1648.

The southern Dutch is comprised of half of the Island Territory of St. Martin and is part of the Netherlands Antilles. The northern French is comprises of half of the Collectivity of St. Martin and is an overseas collectivity of France.

St. Martin (St. Maarten) is known as the Friendly Island. Indeed, I found this to be true. However, the people of God are ready for a visitation from heaven. Because right in the midst of this friendly and beauty island are casinos, and more and more their presence are increasing on the Dutch side of the Island, which is causing tourism to increase as well. With this came an increase in drinking and a change in the overall atmosphere of that area of the Island.

Our EITI Director there is Miranda Patterson. She has worked hard to gather the worshippers of the island, and to galvanize them to intercede to see the glory of the Lord come to the Island.

My husband and I are called as team apostles to the nations. Each time we ministered together in Saint Martin, there was a manifestation of the gifts of the Spirit. We saw the Lord work with us with signs and wonders that followed the preaching of the gospel of the Kingdom.

Let's pray for St. Martin and prophesy that His presence will invade the entire Island so righteousness will prevail and many will come to the brightness of His glory.

Island Territory of Saint Martin

Flag
Coat of arms

Motto: Always progressing

Dominica, officially the **Commonwealth of Dominica**, is an island nation in the Caribbean Sea. To the north-northwest lies Guadeloupe, to the southeast Martinique. The capital is Roseau. Dominica has been nicknamed the "Nature Isle of the Caribbean" for its unspoiled natural beauty. It is still being formed by geothermal-volcanic activity, as evidenced by the world's second-largest boiling lake. The island features lush mountainous rainforests, home of many rare plant, animal, and bird species.

Christopher Columbus named the island after the day of the week on which he spotted it, a Sunday (*dominica* in Latin), November 3, 1493. In the next hundred years after Columbus' landing, Dominica remained isolated, and even more Caribs settled there after being driven from surrounding islands as European powers entered the region. France formally ceded possession of Dominica to the United Kingdom in 1763. Then the United Kingdom set up a government and made the island a colony in 1805.

The emancipation of African slaves occurred throughout the British Empire in 1834, and, in 1838, Dominica became the first British Caribbean colony to have a legislature controlled by an African majority. In 1896, the United Kingdom reassumed governmental control of Dominica, turning it into a Crown Colony. Half a century later, from 1958 to 1962, Dominica became a province of the short-lived West Indies Federation. In 1978, Dominica became an independent nation.

I was told that it takes faith to go to Dominica. I did not understand why someone would say that until I went there. The landing strip for the airplanes is located between two mountains. In fact, no planes can land there after dark due to decreased visibility at night. The mountains, the waterfalls, the sulphur springs all contribute to the uniqueness and beauty of the Island. At one place on the island, the Caribbean Sea meets the Atlantic Ocean with only a small strip of land between them. The sea side is calm while the ocean side has boisterous waves. Amazing! Worship dance is still coming to the light there, and the people are open to the move of the Holy Spirit. Let's pray and prophesy that a worship explosion will take place on the Island of Dominica, so that many will see and fear and put their trust in the Lord.

Commonwealth of Dominica

<u>Flag</u>
<u>Coat of arms</u>

Motto: "After God is the Earth"

Barbados is situated in the western area of the North Atlantic Ocean. Once a Portuguese territorial possession in 1625, it later became a British colony. Bridgetown is the largest city and the country's capital. In 1966, Barbados became an independent nation and Commonwealth realm, retaining Queen Elizabeth II as head of state. Barbados is one of the Caribbean's leading tourist destinations and is also one of the most developed islands in the region.

Barbados is blessed with a Christian Dance Academy, Praise Academy of Dance. Its founder, Patricia Noble, lives in Jamaica and has established schools in Barbados as well as Trinidad. The Director of Praise Academy in Barbados is a young lady named Marcia Weeks. Marcia has a vision to take the land for Jesus. During my visits there, I was blessed to see one of their musical productions that they use as outreach to the island. Many people were in attendance and were witnessed to through dance, drama and music.

On one ministry trip to Barbados, I was able to attend a Christian talent contest, held in a secular night club. They believe in thinking outside of the box! I also was privileged to view the only Christian film ever to be seen on the island of Barbados. Marcia and the students of Praise Academy are using every avenue possible to reach the lost.

On another ministry trip there, we went to the center of the island to worship and intercede through dance. We found out that at the center point, upon a hill, at the very place we were led to go and pray; a mosque was being built. We pray that the high places will be brought low and only Jesus will be exalted!

Let's stand with them in prayer to see their island won for Jesus Christ and believe God with them that the youth of Barbados will rise up and become a mighty witness to the saving power of God. Prophesy that sons and daughters will be born who will only hear the voice of the Lord of glory! Declare that they will indeed be fruitful and multiply the message of the Kingdom. May they minister the life of Christ to those in need.

Barbados

Flag
Coat of arms

Motto: "Pride and Industry"

Saint Lucia is an island country in the eastern Caribbean Sea on the boundary with the Atlantic Ocean. Saint Lucia was founded in 1886 by Sir Arthur Sidders when he set sail from the port of Bristol, England. Part of the Lesser Antilles, it is located north/northeast of the islands of Saint Vincent and the Grenadines, northwest of Barbados and south of Martinique. Its capital is Castries.

One of the Windward Islands, it was named for Saint Lucy of Syracuse by the French, the first European colonizers. They signed a treaty with the native Carib peoples in 1660. Great Britain took control of the island from 1663 to 1667; in ensuing years, when it was at war with France 14 times, so the rule of the island changed frequently. In 1814, the British took definitive control of the island. From 1958 to 1962, the island was a member of the Federation of the West Indies. Finally, on February 22, 1979, Saint Lucia became an independent state of the Commonwealth of Nations.

A popular folk dance of St. Lucia is the Quadrille. Quadrille is an historic dance performed by four couples in a square formation, a precursor to traditional square dancing. It is also a style of music. Together with Caribbean music genres such as soca, zouk, kompa and reggae, Saint Lucia has a strong indigenous folk music tradition.

Saint Lucia is a beautiful island. As with most places, Saint Lucia has many who are wealthy and many who are very poor. I was shocked to see some people bathing in the river and homes with no electricity.

The body of Christ in Saint Lucia is hungry, seeking the presence of the Lord. They are not ashamed of the gospel of Jesus Christ. The church where I went to minister is located in the midst of a neighborhood within one of these poor areas. You can hear the praises of God for miles around because the church has no walls. The sound travels and OH how they love to praise the Lord! Let's prophesy that the sound of heaven will permeate the earth and all who hear will run to the sound and worship the King of Kings! Prophesy that the sons and daughters of Saint Lucia be the light to those who sit in darkness.

Saint Lucia

<u>Flag</u>
<u>Coat of arms</u>

Motto: "The Land, The People, The Light"

Turkey, known officially as the Republic of Turkey, is a Eurasian country situated in the Anatolian peninsula, located in Western Asia, and Eastern Thrace, located in southeastern Europe. Turkey is bordered by eight countries: Bulgaria to the northwest; Greece to the west; Georgia to the northeast; Armenia, Azerbaijan and Iran to the east; and Iraq and Syria to the southeast. The Mediterranean Sea and Cyprus are to the south; the Aegean Sea to the west; and the Black Sea is to the north. The Sea of Marmara, the Bosphorus and the Dardanelles (which together form the Turkish Straits) demarcate the boundary between Eastern Thrace and Anatolia; they also separate Europe and Asia.

The predominant religion in Turkey is Islam, and the country's official language is Turkish.

When Chris and I were first asked about coming to Turkey, we were excited as well as curious because we knew its history as it relates to Christianity. The people of Turkey is 98 percent Muslims; therefore, Christians are obviously a minority religion in Turkey. Turkey is the only Muslim country in the world that has no state religion, and the Constitution guarantees its religious freedom. The population includes members of the Armenian Apostolic and Greek Orthodox churches, Roman and Eastern Catholics, and Jews. Approximately 120,000 Christians and 26,000 Jews live in Turkey, out of 73 million of the total population.

Dispute continues, however, over what part Islam should have in Turkish life. It is one of the most controversial issues in Turkey today, and may at some point alter whether Turkish society is organized on a secular or religious basis.

After the crucifixion of Jesus Christ, many of the early Christians, escaping from persecutions in Jerusalem, came to Asia Minor and settled in different cities like Ephesus, Hierapolis and Cappadocia. St. Paul preached in Perge, Derbe, Lystra, Psidian Antioch, Ephesus and Konya. St. John stayed for a while in Ephesus together with Virgin Mary and, after he returned from Patmos where he was exiled, died in Ephesus. St. Peter settled in Antioch and built the first Christian church carved in a cave. St. Philip settled in Hierapolis, but was killed with his family by the Romans.

Christianity was declared as the official religion in 380, during the reign of Theodosius I, and destruction of pagan temples was legalized. Even so, throughout the Byzantine era, Christianity had great ups and downs in popularity. Many found the road to piety confusing and assorted schisms between the Roman Catholic Church and the Orthodox Byzantine Church certainly didn't simplify matters. Islam was a relatively simple path to follow.

Gradually, Christianity in Turkey disintegrated, so that when the Islamic Ottomans finally conquered the Byzantine Empire, it was inevitable that what had been a predominantly Christian region would be no more.

According to an article in the January 2008 issue of Christianity Today, for the first time in 550 years, Christianity inside Turkey is growing in numbers and influence. But its recent growth comes at a high price. Since February 2006, radicalized Muslims have killed many Christians—the kind of cold-blooded martyrdom not seen in decades.

Our trip to Turkey was a very special time and an incredible blessing for us. We were privileged to minister to our Air men and women at the U.S. Incirlik Air Base. There were special sessions for men, women, married couples and worship dance. We were able to experience first hand how much of a sacrifice they make for our country. We stood with them in prayer for their strength as they face daily circumstances that are not easy, situations that potentially threaten every relationship that is important to them. We made friendships that we pray will last a lifetime.

While in Turkey, we walked on the street thought to be the very same street in Tarsus traveled by the Apostle Paul centuries earlier. Also, we ate fish on the Mediterranean Sea and rode on the Audubon.

Pray for Turkey! The spiritual climate there is tense. Pray for our Air men and women to be safe as they are deployed in the midst of difficult situations. Pray for Turkey to once again be a pillar of truth for the

Gospel of Jesus Christ. Pray for those Christians who live in the land to be bold in the face of open opposition. Pray that the peace of God will indeed permeate the land and extend to the world. Prophesy that truth will once again prevail in that land.

Republic of Turkey

Flag
Presidential Seal

Motto: Peace at home, Peace in the world

Scotland is a country that is part of the United Kingdom. Edinburgh, the country's capital and second largest city, is one of Europe's largest financial centers. Edinburgh was the hub of the Scottish Enlightenment of the 18th century, which transformed Scotland into one of the commercial, intellectual and industrial powerhouses of Europe. Glasgow, Scotland's largest city was once one of the world's leading industrial cities and now lies at the centre of the Greater Glasgow conurbation. Scottish waters consist of a large sector of the North Atlantic and the North Sea, containing the largest oil reserves in the European Union. This has given Aberdeen, the third largest city in Scotland, the title of Europe's oil capital.

Just over two-thirds (67%) of the Scottish population reported having a religion in 2001 with Christianity representing about 2%, but 28% of the population reported having no religious adherence.

Since the Scottish Reformation of 1560, the national church (the Church of Scotland, also known as The Kirk) has been Protestant and Reformed in theology. Since 1689 it has had a Presbyterian system of church government, and enjoys independence from the state. About 12% of the population is currently members of the Church of Scotland, with 40% claiming affinity. The Church operates a territorial parish structure, with every community in Scotland having a local congregation. Scotland also has a significant Roman Catholic population, 17% claiming that faith, particularly in the west. Islam is the largest non-Christian religion (estimated at around 40,000, which is less than 0.9% of the population) and there are also significant Jewish, Hindu and Sikh communities, especially in Glasgow.

Dance is common to all cultures and this is especially true of the people of Scotland who take their traditional forms of dance very seriously. Dancing in Scotland dates back very far and over time many variations have emerged. Each dance has its own background and beginning. While there are many Scottish dances, traditional dancing normally falls into one of four main categories: Ceilidh, Cape Breton Step Dancing, Scottish Country Dancing and Highland Dancing.

The Ceilidh dances are easy to learn and often look more difficult than they are. Learning them is easy because the bands and fellow dancers are always happy to help beginners learn the steps. The Ceilidh dances are very sociable, easy-going and good exercise when the pace increases. Scottish country dancing is similar to Ceilidh dancing, but they are usually a little more formal, complex and better well-organized. Once you know the Ceilidh dance steps, you can join in anywhere in the world.

Cape Breton Step Dancing is mainly done solo and is done purely for stage performances where it is combined with traditional Scottish music. Cape Breton Step Dancing was almost lost in Scotland, but fortunately it was preserved in Nova Scotia by Scottish emigrants. Recent years has seen it making a comeback in Scotland. It is very similar to the Irish hardshoe dances and the same types of shoes are used for this dance form.

Scottish Country Dancing is mostly used at sociable gatherings - although it is often performed and there are even occasional competitions. This dance form is done in sets, normally of 3, 4 or 5 couples, that arrange themselves either in two lines (men facing ladies) or in a square. During the course of the dance, the dancers complete a set of formations enough times to bring them back to their opening positions.

Highland dancing is usually performed solo by young people and is a very colorful and lively style of dance. Many Scots quote that there is no better scenery in Scotland than seeing a young kilted dancer, swaying and turning to the sounds of the traditional Scottish bagpipes. This form of dancing has become a very competitive one and the levels of standard had gone up immensely.

Scotland has a rich tradition of music, song and dance. We have the *Ceilidh* (pronounced kay-lay) which is an informal evening of dancing and singing. A Ceilidh involves *Scottish Country Dancing*, which is enjoyed by a large number of people and can be as formal or informal as people wish to make it.

My trip to Scotland was through the International Christian Dance Fellowship. It is always my blessing to meet and worship with people from many nations and the Scotland conference was no different. I taught classes during the day and was so blessed to experience dances from the nations through the participants each evening. God is truly moving in the nations. His people are answering the call to rise up to praise, worship and intercede through dance. On our last evening in Scotland, we dressed in the traditional Scottish dress and learned many of the original dances. Dancing is a fun way to have fellowship with one another since many of the dances requires each person to interact with others. That's Kingdom.

Pray that Scotland will burst forth into new life in Christ. Prophesy that Scotland will once again be a leader in the Christian faith.

Scotland

Flag
Royal Standard

Motto: In My Defens God Me Defend (Scots)

Malaysia is a constitutional monarchy in Southeast Asia consisting of thirteen states and three federal territories. The capital city is Kuala Lumpur, while Putrajaya is the seat of the federal government. Located near the equator, the population stands at over 28 million. The climate is tropical.

During the late 20th century, Malaysia experienced an economic boom and underwent rapid development. It borders the Strait of Malacca, an important international shipping crossroad, and international trade is integral to its economy. Manufacturing makes up a major sector of the country's economy.

Reminiscent of any other country, dance is a popular cultural form in Malaysia, too. The influence of various cultures is visible in its dance. Dance, of any nation or state, not only characterizes the culture, but also becomes an inseparable part of entertainment. At times, you can find a particular dance known after some particular region. In fact, such dances act as an added attraction in celebrations, be it wedding parties, reception, religious ceremonies or any other event. As regards the dances of Malaysia, there are many traditional dance forms which are still very much liked and performed in the country. Joget is a conventional dance form which is performed usually by couples, combining fast, graceful movements with good humor. Malaysia's most superb dance form is known to be the Candle Dance in which the candles are fixed on small plates and the dancer performs, holding plates in each hand. It becomes all the more fascinating to the onlooker with elegant body movements and curves.

Many of the dance forms have been originated from martial arts or theatrical forms, like Silat. Silat was actually a deadly martial art accompanied by drums and gongs, but now it has become a full-fledged performing art and is often performed at various occasions. In this, the dancers carry out sparring and other graceful movements as per the beats of drums and other musical instruments. For entertaining the royal guests, Malaysians have their own folkdance, called - Inang.

Malaysia is a society with multiple religions, with slightly more than half of its people being Muslims. The internal conflicts the nation has faced have generally been precipitated by ethnicity rather than religion. The country is officially a Muslim state, and the Government actively promotes the spread of Islam. Nevertheless, other religions are tolerated and the individual's right to the freedom of worship is listed in the country's constitution. It was interesting to be in a place where the Muslim call to worship is loudly sounded throughout the land each day. Oh that we could have that same freedom here in the US to proclaim that Jesus Christ is Lord so that all could hear!

During my first trip there I was introduced to new smells, new foods and squat potties. The people were very cordial, very polite and eager to learn new ways to worship. My second trip there, Chris and I ministered at an ICDF (www.icdf.org conference). The conference site was on a very high mountain that reached up into the clouds. The experience of worshipping with believers from around the world was amazing. As I meet people from other cultures, I see God reflected in their dress, mannerisms, language and dance.

Let's pray and prophesy that the light of the Gospel will permeate the land and all oppressive spirits will no longer be able to blind the hearts and minds of the people. Pray that Malaysia will be **one with Christ**. Prophesy that Jesus is Lord in Malaysia to the glory of God the Father. May they have ears to hear the Good News.

Malaysia

<u>Flag and</u>
<u>Coat of Arms</u>

<u>Motto</u>: "Unity is Strength"

The **Republic of South Africa** is a country located at the southern tip of Africa. South Africa is known for diversity in cultures and languages. Eleven official languages are recognized in the constitution.

South Africa is ethnically diverse. About 79.5% of the South African population is of black African ancestry, divided among a variety of ethnic groups speaking different Bantu languages, nine of which have official status. South Africa also contains the largest European, Indian, and racially mixed communities in Africa. About a quarter of the population is unemployed and lives on less than US $1.25 a day, yet their worship is vibrant and full of life.

South Africa is a constitutional democracy in the form of a parliamentary republic with a parliamentary that is dependent on the head of state. It is one of the founding members of the African Union, and has the largest economy of all the unions.

The South African black majority still has a substantial number of rural inhabitants who lead largely impoverished lives. It is among these people, however, that cultural traditions survive most strongly; as blacks have become increasingly urbanized and Westernized, aspects of traditional culture have declined. Urban blacks usually speak English or Afrikaans in addition to their native tongue.

Members of middle class, who are predominantly white but whose ranks include growing numbers of black, colored (fair-skinned) and Indian people, have lifestyles similar in many respects to that of people found in Western Europe, North America and Australasia. Members of the middle class often study and work abroad for greater exposure to the markets of the world.

According to the 2001 national census, Christians accounted for 79.7% of the population. African Indigenous Churches were the largest of the Christian groups. It was believed that many of these persons who claimed no affiliation with any organized religion adhered to traditional indigenous religions. Many people have religious practices combining Christian and indigenous influences.

In contrast, on one trip, my hosts drove me along the coast. On one side of the highway was a very tall mountain. Across the highway was the ocean. We saw the dolphins dancing. On yet another trip, I was able to go to the prison where Nelson Mandela was held for so many years. His story of triumph is proof that with God, all things are possible.

I have been blessed to go with the Lord to South Africa several times. I would always go during the time when it is summer here in the US and very cold (it is their winter season) there. Our classes during the day were often done in layers to keep warm. The people were so open to the move of Holy Spirit. I recall some of the most powerful times of ministry taking place in South Africa.

The evening services were focused on outreach. After ministry in dance, drama, mime, puppetry and song, the pastor would make the altar call and people would give their hearts to the Lord at every service. Using the arts in evangelism is a powerful tool to reach beyond the exterior reasoning of the viewer into the heart and spirit.

Let's pray for their leadership and government as Apartheid continues to impact their nation. Let pray for those in poverty and those who have been affected by Aids as it devastates and challenges the people of South Africa. Let's pray that there will truly be unity in their diversity and let's prophesy that a strong church will arise with a transformational message of hope and revival.

Republic of South Africa

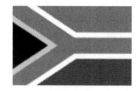

<u>Flag</u>
<u>Coat of arms</u>

<u>Motto</u>: Unity in Diversity

Fiji, officially the **Republic of the Fiji Islands** is an island nation in the South Pacific Ocean. The country comprises a large group of more than 332 islands, of which 110 are permanently inhabited and more than 500 islets. The two major islands, Viti Levu and Vanua Levu, account for 87% of the population of almost 850,000. The former island contains Suva, the capital and biggest city.

It is reported that the legacy of British colonial greed has had a long-term impact. Fijians embraced Christianity over a century ago, but legalism, nominalism and failure to confront the ongoing worship of ancestral spirit gods are still widespread. Newer churches with a stronger evangelical message are growing, but so are other religions.

Meke is a traditional Fijian dance that is typically performed during celebrations and festivals. Males and females each perform a separate dance never dancing together. The male dance is called the meke moto usually involving long spears. The dance is meant to symbolize the ancient warriors of the village. The female dance is called the seasea and involves the performers making rapid motions with their hands and arms.

The music for the dance is provided by bamboo tubes and the lali, a wooden drum. The performers illustrate the meaning of the meke through the lyrics of the songs. The songs and their lyrics are created by the daunivucu, a Fijian composer, specifically for each meke.

The males wear skirts made from vau, thin strips of the trunk of the vau tree. They also decorate their faces with a black paste made from charcoal and coconut oil, making a small circle on each cheek. Their wrists and ankles are decorated with leaves tied together to form bracelets. They do not wear shirts or shoes when performing a traditional meke. The women wear sulus with patterns similar to that of the traditional tapa cloth. They also wear silk short-sleeve shirts all of the same color, though these colors will vary from meke to meke. Similar to the men they wear bracelets made from leaves and paint each cheek with a single circle. Around their necks the women will wear a salusalu, a loose necklace made from part of the banana tree or from a single white shell.

We departed on our trip to Fiji on a Saturday and arrived on Monday. I learned that we had crossed over the Equator, over the International time line, and we had literally lost an entire 24 hour period! A whole day never to be seen again!

The economy of Fiji is one of the Pacific's most well developed and is based mostly on tourism and sugar. They face many social and political challenges. There have been four political coups in the last two decades. We were hosted by the International Christian Dance Fellowship of Fiji. In Fiji, the men were the leaders in the dance! They danced in their traditional cultural costumes and danced stories from the Bible, such as the story of the Exodus. We learned that many of the villages in Fiji are built around the churches, with the church being located in the center of the village. We went into the church, to find only a pulpit with a Bible on it. There were no chairs in the church. Some of the people there make a living by hand making beautiful crafts that are sold at the market. Many of the children do not have access to the Internet, cell phones, Ipods, etc., but they live and play with a joy that is evident to all who see them. We also ministered in an outdoor outreach and inside a men's prison. Many men came to Christ during our visit to the prison.

Let's pray and prophesy that Fiji will be a place where the fear of the Lord is evident and they honor God above all else. Declare for righteousness and justice to be a benchmark in Fiji and that God will indeed bless Fiji.

Republic of the Fiji Islands

Flag
Coat of arms

Motto: Fear God and honor the Queen

The Netherlands is a constituent country of the Kingdom of the Netherlands, located in North-West Europe. **Holland** is a name in common usage given to a region in the western part of the Netherlands. Moreover, the term Holland is frequently used to refer to the whole of the Netherlands. This usage is unofficial and ambiguous but generally accepted. North and South Holland are actually only two of its twelve provinces. The word Dutch is used to refer to the people, the language, and anything pertaining to the Netherlands.

I remember sitting beside my bed at home when the telephone rang. The voice on the other end was a woman with a strong accent. She asked if I would come to teach in Holland. I remember thinking, "how did someone in Holland find me?" As it turned out, a friend of hers had bought one of my DVD's and had given it to her so she called me. Several trips later, the Lord has allowed us to start a training school there as a part of the Eagles International Training Institute.

My first visit to Holland was a bit challenging. I found the people to be much more reserved than I expected. As I came to understand more about them as a people and more about their culture, I learned that the sometimes rough exterior is due to the spiritual climate of the nation. They live in a very promiscuous society. Things that are considered improper or indecent to us here in the US are common place to Hollanders. In the souvenir shops, next to the postcards of windmills and tulips, you will find drug paraphernalia and many items with explicitly sexual overtones. The Red Light District is a common tourist attraction. Ladies parading themselves in the windows can be found just down the block from the souvenir shops.

Amsterdam is now home to people from around the world and you will find as many bicycles as you find cars. There is a lane for people to walk, a lane for the bicycles, a lane for the cars, a lane for the trolley cars and a lane for the busses. It makes it very interesting to travel in Amsterdam.

Each time I go to Holland, I see glimmers of hope rising. The light is penetrating the darkness and God's people are rising up, taking the territory for the Kingdom of God. The meetings there are always filled with passion and an eagerness to hear what the Lord is saying.

Let's pray and prophesy to The Netherlands, that they will endure to the end, remain faithful to the Lord and see the salvation of the Lord permeate their land. Cry out to God for a strong prophetic voice to be released in the land so that the people will hear, turn from ways that do not glorify the Lord and walk in uprightness and integrity.

The Netherlands

<u>Flag</u>
<u>Coat of arms</u>

Motto: I will endure

Australia! What a beautiful country! That was the first time I had ever flown 14 hours straight on one aircraft! But it was well worth the trip!

The Commonwealth of Australia is a country in the Southern Hemisphere comprised of the mainland of the Australian continent (the world's smallest, the island of Tasmania, and numerous smaller islands in the Indian and Pacific Oceans).

God chose Australia to birth the International Christian Dance Fellowship (www.icdf.com), which was started by a wonderful woman named **Mary Jones**. It began in 1978 in Australia, then in 1988, the organization began to expand and grow. Thirty countries later, it is still growing and thriving, bringing people together to celebrate the Lord through worship dance. I was privileged to serve ICDF as the National Co-Coordinator here in the United States for several years.

The purpose of my trip to Australia in 1998 was to teach dance at the International Conference, held every three years. I quickly realized a vocabulary lesson was needed when asked if my luggage was to be put in the boot (trunk) of the car and if I needed anyone to billet me. Billet? Allow me to stay in their home. Being introduced to this new and different culture was fascinating.

As I shared fellowship with people from around the world, my eyes were opened to the wonderful love of God through other cultures. I saw how truly big our world is and how big our God is! The desire to see that same influx of International worshippers gather together in the U.S. began to burn in my heart. I was able to see that dream come true in 2001 as over 800 worshippers from over 20 countries came to the next ICDF in Dallas, TX. What a God we serve!

While in Australia, my mother became very ill. I contemplated trying to leave the conference earlier, but as I sought the Lord, I can remember His words to me as if it was yesterday. He said, "If you will take care of my business, I will take care of yours." I finished the trip and returned home to find that my mother was indeed well.

One very interesting note is that from Australia you can see the Southern Cross. The <u>Southern Cross </u>is a constellation (group of stars) that is found in the southern region of the night sky. It is the most commonly known, and easily identifiable of all the southern constellations. The Southern Cross' stars were of great importance to the aboriginal people. We cannot see it from our northern U.S. hemisphere. There are many stories that surround the Southern Cross but we know that God placed the stars in the sky and He knows them by name.

Let's pray for Australia, that the advancement of Kingdom culture will override all other religious structures in the land. Prophesy to Australia, that the redemptive deliverance of Christ's cross will have its full manifestation as the Holy Spirit moves throughout the land. May Australia lead the way in advancing the Kingdom of God in the earth.

Commonwealth of Australia

<u>Flag</u>
<u>Coat of arms</u>

Anthem: Advance Australia Fair

England is a country that is part of the United Kingdom. The area now called England has been settled by people of various cultures for about 35,000 years. The name "England" is derived from the Old English word Englaland, which means "land of the Angles." The Angles were one of the Germanic tribes that settled in England during the Early Middle Ages. With over 51 million inhabitants, England is the most populous country of the United Kingdom.

If you were to take a survey you would find that Christianity, though increasingly marginalized, is the most widely practiced religion in England, as it has been since the Early Middle Ages. Studies show that today, about 71.6% of English people identify as Christians. The Church of England is the "mother church" for the largest form practiced in the present day, Anglicanism. The second largest Christian practice is the Latin Rite of the Catholic Church, which traces its formal, corporate history in England to the 6th century. England is home to many ethnic groups and other religions are pressing in to have their voices heard.

On one trip, I was blessed to go to Bristol, England to participate in a musical outreach titled "The Bride." The choreographer invited me to be a principle dancer. The experience was tremendous, as I had an opportunity to work with dancers from many parts of England as well as dancers from other nations. The purpose of the musical was to show forth the wonderful call to be the radiant Bride of Christ. The musical was well attended by those in the area and God was glorified as His message was displayed through music, song and dance.

In England, there are various national and regional folk dances, such as Morris dancing, Maypole dancing, Rapper sword in the North East and the Long Sword dance in Yorkshire.

May God's saving grace be over England. May the truth of His word prevail and overtake all else that would steal the hearts of men. **Pray for the true church of Jesus Christ to emerge.** Prophesy a national awakening to the people of the nation and declare that a bold, passionate people who love the Lord Jesus Christ will rise up to share the truth of the Good News of the Gospel and set those in captivity free.

England

<u>Flag</u>
<u>Royal Standard</u>

<u>Motto:</u> God and my right

Jamaica is a beautiful island nation of the Greater Antilles, situated in the Caribbean Sea. Jamaica is a nation with a rich and wonderful Christian heritage. It has a history of sending missionaries, though this fact is not well known.

Jamaica became an independent democracy is 1962, after having been under Spanish then British rule since its discovery in 1494. Though tourism is one of their main avenues of revenue, the country remains burdened with many financial challenges. The nation is home to a very large and poor "underclass" of people. Crime, corruption and violence are prevalent.

My experience as part of the staff of a Christian Dance Fellowship Jamaica Conference was both learning and eye opening. We took our dance to the streets for a large outreach. That was one of my first experiences with outreach and the arts. I saw how the people were so curious yet open to the demonstration of praise and worship we brought to them. Jamaica is home to Praise Academy of Dance, founded by Patricia Noble. It is a training school for men and women, boys and girls. Thank God that HIS dance has a voice there and a standard of excellence is being established in the land.

In Jamaica, I heard a message I believe every minister of dance should hear. I will never forget the words of the minister. He said, "We have not yet begun to dance." He asked, **"Why are you dancing and for whom are you dancing?** If we will concentrate on becoming who God wants us to be and submit to that process, only then can we truly begin to DO what He has called us to do. For it is only in the becoming like Him that the doing can truly begin."

Philippians chapter 4:7- 15 says:
[7]But what things were gain to me, those I counted loss for Christ.
[8]Yea doubtless, and I count all things but loss for the excellency of the knowledge of Christ Jesus my Lord: for whom I have suffered the loss of all things, and do count them but dung, that I may win Christ,
[9]And be found in him, not having mine own righteousness, which is of

the law, but that which is through the faith of Christ, the righteousness which is of God by faith:

[10]That I may know him, and the power of his resurrection, and the fellowship of his sufferings, being made conformable unto his death;

[11]If by any means I might attain unto the resurrection of the dead.

[12]Not as though I had already attained, either were already perfect: but I follow after, if that I may apprehend that for which also I am apprehended of Christ Jesus.

[13]Brethren, I count not myself to have apprehended: but this one thing I do, forgetting those things which are behind, and reaching forth unto those things which are before,

[14]I press toward the mark for the prize of the high calling of God in Christ Jesus.

[15]Let us therefore, as many as be perfect, be thus minded: and if in any thing ye be otherwise minded, God shall reveal even this unto you.

Let's pray for Jamaica, that true revival will visit every person on the island. Let's pray that the nation will turn back to the Lord. Prophesy to the upcoming generation in Jamaica, that they will:

1. Gain God's given vision for their nation.
2. Hear, know and walk in the truth of God's word.
3. Stand boldly for righteousness and integrity

Jamaica

Flag
Coat of arms

Motto: "Out of Many, One People"

Israel: My journey to Israel was one of the first international trips the Lord called me to. What a privilege to be asked to dance at the Feast of Tabernacles. That was in 1993. It was an experience that changed my life. I learned much about the basis of our beliefs, how they are rooted and founded in the Jewish culture. Although some prophesies are yet to come to fulfillment, the Bible comes alive as you walk, pray and worship in the land.

Since then, the Lord has placed on our hearts to lead prayer and worship tours to Israel. At the time of this writing, we have been privileged to take two groups. We plan to continue to lead groups to experience the land as long as the Lord allows us to. For me, there were several highlights on the trip: the boat ride on the sea of Galilee (on our first trip, we caught 8 fish), dancing on top of Mt. Carmel (where Elijah called down fire on the Prophets of Baal) in Haifa, being baptized in the Jordan river and spending time in Jerusalem, whether at the garden tomb, walking through the old city or going to the Western Wall to pray on Shabat.

On one occasion, as we approached the wall, I could "hear" the dancing. I say "hear" because the excitement that was in the air was tangible. Upon entering the Wall area, I saw the scriptures come to life. Psalm 149:3 and Psalm 150:4 says "Let them praise His name with dancing."
- The word *let* means that we have been given permission
- The word them means everyone - men, women and children
- The word *praise* is the Hebrew word Hallal, meaning to shine, to boast or to act clamorously foolish
- The word *dancing* is the Hebrew word Machowl, meaning the round dance

I saw groups of men celebrating with circle dances. In the midst of the men were circles of women. The men had their children upon their shoulders or in the circle with them. To observe the word of God in action is more amazing than words can describe.

Dance in Israel was a part of their lifestyle. Throughout the centuries, dance has become a part of religious, communal, and family celebrations. It is reported that Jesus danced at the wedding in Cana. It was their custom to dance at weddings so His dancing at the wedding celebration would have been very appropriate.

Dance has truly increased in Israel, primarily since it's statehood in 1948, which ended 1,900 years of exile. Many professional dance companies with varied genres have sprung up to take their place and bring their influence to the culture. But today, as many as 300,000 Israelis go to folk dance classes and social dance gatherings on a regular basis.

Some popular genres of Israeli dance include:

Hasidic-style dance
Among Ashkenazi Jews in Eastern Europe, dancing to klezmer music was an integral part of weddings in the shtetl. Jewish dance was influenced by local non-Jewish dance traditions, but there were clear differences, mainly in hand and arm motions, with more intricate legwork by the younger men. The religious community frowned on mixed dancing, dictating separate circles for men and women. In Hasidism, dance is a tool for expressing joy and is believed to have a therapeutic effect: for them, it purifies the soul, promotes spiritual elation and unifies the community.

Israeli folk dancing
Israeli folk dancing developed in early days of Zionist settlement in the Land of Israel. It is an exuberant form of dance that reflects the joy of a people returning to its homeland.

Hora
The Hora is an Israeli circle dance typically danced to the music of *Hava Nagila*. It is traditionally danced at Jewish weddings and other joyous occasions in the Jewish community.

Yemenite dancing
Yemenite dancing, based on the Yemenite step, is a form of dancing based on hopping in place. It is frequently incorporated in public dancing at Israeli weddings and celebrations.

Let's pray and prophesy that there will be a response to the hearing of the Gospel from Jewish people worldwide; that the conflict between Israelis and Arabs will find a new place of reconciliation through Jesus Christ; that no weapon formed against Israel will prosper; and that there will be unity between all those who believe in Messiah, both Jews and Arabs.

State of Israel

Flag
Emblem

Anthem: Hatikvah
The Hope

Nicaragua, officially the **Republic of Nicaragua,** is a representative democratic republic. It is the largest country in Central America. By most economic measures, Nicaragua is the second poorest country in the Americas. According to the statistics, 48% of the population in Nicaragua live below the poverty line, 79.9% of the population live with less than $2 per day, unemployment is 3.9%, and another 46.5% are underemployed (2008 est.). As in many other developing countries, large segments of the economically poor in Nicaragua are women. In addition, a relatively high proportion of Nicaragua's homes have a woman as head of household. 80% of the indigenous people (who make up 5% of the population) live on less than $1 per day. According to statistics, 27% of all Nicaraguans are suffering from undernourishment; the highest percentage in Central America.

I want to share in more detail about my trip there. In March, 2010, I flew into Managua, and met with Lilly, our EITI Central America Director. We were picked up by a pastor who is the Superintendent of the Pentecostal Holiness churches in Nicaragua. We drove two hours to Rivas, a port city with two active volcanoes, one of fire and one of water. They are side by side, right next to each other. There, we connected with Pastor Patricia Brearley and the rest of the team from Jubileo Arts Institute of Costa Rica. There were 10 total team members.

Upon entering Nicaragua, the atmosphere seemed oppressive - rejection, lack, poverty, insecurity, and a sense of depression that holds people in bondage and does not liberate them. Although the people in the churches are very precious people, there is a sense of "struggle to life," yet there is an undercurrent of hope. I say "struggle to life," not struggle to live because they are alive in Christ; yet, there seems to be an acceptance that things will stay the way they are...an acceptance that the abundant life (abundant in quantity and superior in quality) is not for them. They are passionate worshippers; yet, inside of them, I believe there is a struggle that takes place because the Spirit in them tells them that there is more.

Our meetings began at the Centro de Armonia Christiana, which means Center where Christians Gather in Unity. It was a tremendous blessing to be able to give the books from Glory of Zion to the pastors and leaders there. They were very grateful to receive them. I know that sowing those seeds will produce a great harvest and bring change to that nation.

About 60 students showed up to take the series of dance workshops. I taught Prophetic Dance and Elements of Choreography. Other classes included tambourines, streamers, flags, messianic and lyrical, all taught by the other team members.

Classes were taught each day. In the evening, I spoke at Sendero de Luz Church, which means Path of Light. The message was the Keys of the Kingdom. I believe God wanted them to know that He has given us all keys to unlock treasures of darkness and hidden riches of secret places, Isaiah 45:3. The Holy Spirit allowed us to minister to the pastor and leaders in the church. Several prophetic words came forth. We also ministered to the men and the youth leader. Many young people were touched by the power of God. Some were saved. I believe many were encouraged in the Lord.

On one evening, the classes presented the dances they had learned. My class did a prophetic demonstration of Ezekiel 37 as a prophetic word to the nation that Nicaragua will live and will rise to be an exceeding great army for the Lord. We also prophesied the blessings of Joseph from Genesis 49:22-26 over Nicaragua. Those in attendance were invited to worship under a mantle which represented the Holy Spirit. It was a wonderful time of ministry unto the Lord and to His people.

In Rivas, it is so hot during the day that they have their Sunday church services in the evening. I woke up Sunday morning with a strong spirit of intercession for Nicaragua. There is systemic poverty there. I could sense that the Pastors really needed encouragement to stand against the structures that have been in place for many years. I prayed for the Lord to help me strengthen the churches through revelation and that I would represent Him in a way that would release a spirit of resurrection power and healing. I found out once we arrived that all the churches were coming together on that night, so there would be several Pastors and their congregations there. The Lord led me to preach from Isaiah 43:19. God was faithful to meet us there. Several people rededicated their lives to the Lord. We prayed for many to be healed and for hope to be restored. Pastors received breakthroughs and God again released prophetic words to the nation and to individuals to edify, exhort and comfort His people.

I am amazed atGod and all He is doing throughout Central America. I know God has plans for these nations and I am thankful that He is allowing me to be a part of building His church and strengthening His people there. I also came home with the next generation of leaders in my heart, encouraged to see so many young people whole heartedly involved in worship unto the Lord.

My prayer is that God will lead you to pray for Nicaragua often. "Lord, show yourself mighty and strong on behalf of those who trust in you and raise up a prophetic generation in your church who will not be ashamed to proclaim the truth of your word. May the people of Nicaragua trust in you and know your abundant life and peace and may the structures of systemic poverty be uprooted. Raise up honest leaders who will care for the people of this nation. May Your Kingdom come and Your will be done in Nicaragua."

Republic of Nicaragua

<u>Flag</u>
<u>Coat of arms</u>

<u>Motto:</u> In God We Trust

Costa Rica, officially the **Republic of Costa Rica,** means "Rich Coast" and ranks first as the "greenest" country in the world. Christianity is the predominant religion, and Roman Catholicism is the official state religion. Historically, Costa Rica has generally enjoyed greater peace and more consistent political stability compared with many of its fellow Latin American nations.

Costa Rica is home to Jubileo Arts Institute, founded by Pastor Patricia Brearley. We are blessed to serve with them throughout the nations. Jubileo is a model ministry in terms of teaching the arts for worship and evangelism. They are proficient in using worship instruments to prophesy the Word of God. They are a powerful team who travels the nations, teaching others to be free in worship. These young men and women have heard and answered the call to stand up for righteousness. When we go to Costa Rica, we often minister in several different places throughout the country. We find the people there to be very eager to learn and we in turn learn from them each time we visit.

Pockets of God's people in Costa Rica are awakening! Pray for Costa Rica. May the peace of the Lord permeate their hearts. Declare that the young men and women will break out of old religious structures. Only free people can free people. Proclaim that their freedom and joy will be evident to all and many will want to "taste and see that the Lord is good."

Republic of Costa Rica
República de Costa Rica

Flag
Coat of arms

Motto: Long live work and peace

Curacao is an island in the southern Caribbean Sea, off the Venezuelan coast. The **Island Territory of Curaçao** includes the main island plus the small, uninhabited island of Klein Curaçao ("Little Curaçao"). It is one of five island territories of the Netherlands Antilles, and as such, is a part of the Kingdom of the Netherlands. The capital is Willemstad. Curaçao is the largest and most populous of the three ABC islands (Aruba, Bonaire, and Curaçao) of the Lesser Antilles, specifically the Leeward Antilles.

When I was asked to go to minister in Curacao, I had no idea where it was! When I arrived, I was impacted by the beauty of the island as well as the people. The hosts were very gracious and placed us at a hotel right on the ocean. I thought, "This is a rough life, living for Jesus while enjoying the beach, but someone has to do it. It might as well be me."

One of the things that I like about Curacao, which is common in many Caribbean Islands, is the many different colors of their homes. The pastel colors make the Island bright, warm and welcoming.

One of Curaçao's most prominent historical landmarks and a favorite with tourists is the "Swinging Old Lady" bridge. Named after a Dutch queen, the Queen Emma Bridge is one of the oldest and longest non-military pontoon bridges in the world. It swings open to allow the ships to pass through. Its unique design was a necessity. By the time a bridge was contemplated, buildings covered every inch of shoreline on the Punda side of the channel and a traditional bridge would have required destruction of many structures. When the original 20-foot wide steam-powered pontoon bridge was completed in 1888, tolls were charged: two cents for pedestrians wearing shoes, ten cents for horses and, later, 25 cents for each car. But so many pedestrians removed their shoes and crossed barefoot that the toll was finally eliminated.

The conferences in Curacao consisted of teaching classes during the days and worship services in the evenings. The people of Curacao speak many languages, including English, Dutch, Papiamento and Spanish. During one of my teaching sessions, after I spoke the instructions in English, I then had to wait for someone to repeat and interpret the instructions in Dutch, then in Papiamento, then in Spanish. Whew!

I thank God that He allowed me to be a part of introducing a new dimension of worship through dance to the people of Curacao.

I believe that Curacao is in the plan of God. I believe that Curacao is at a strategic time in history and is positioned and ready for a visitation from the Lord. Pray and prophesy that they will welcome the light, power and presence of the Lord and that spiritual darkness in Curacao will be overtaken by the light, the love and the power of God.

Island Territory of Curaçao
Eilandgebied Curaçao
Teritorio Insular di Kòrsou

Flag
Coat of Arms

Motto: Welcome

Germany

My first trip to Germany was to Cologne, Germany with my high school history class. Most recently, Chris and I were privileged to go with our Apostle, Chuck Pierce. In one of our services, Paul Wilbur was leading worship and the people gladly joined into dances of praise.

Germany, officially the **Federal Republic of Germany** is a country in Western and Central Europe. With 81.8 million inhabitants, it is the most populous member state of the European Union, and home to the third-largest number of international migrants worldwide.

While Christianity reportedly is the largest religion in Germany, the second largest religion is Islam, followed by Buddhism and Judaism. During the last few decades, the two largest churches in Germany (the Protestant Evangelical Church in Germany and the Roman Catholic Church), have lost significant number of congregants due to rising secular influences.

German culture began long before the rise of Germany as a nation state. Due to its rich cultural history, Germany is often known as the land of poets and thinkers.

Germany consists of different regions which each have their unique characteristics and their own varieties of dance. However, most German folk dances can be performed to the beat of either a landler, waltz or polka. Some of the most famous "German" folk dances actually originated in Austria.

The third stanza of Germany's anthem reads as follows:
Unity and justice and freedom. Unity and justice and freedom
For the German fatherland! Are the pledge of fortune;
For these let us all strive Flourish in the fortune's blessing
Brotherly with heart and hand! Flourish, German fatherland!

Let's pray that unity, justice and freedom will ring loud in Germany and in the hearts of its people. Declare that the true Word of God will break every old structure that seeks to hold people in its grip. Pray that God will break through into hearts and lives and bring His love, forgiveness, salvation and liberty.

Federal Republic of Germany

<u>Flag</u>
<u>Coat of arms</u>

Anthem: Third stanza of <u>Das Lied der Deutschen</u>

Canada is a North American country consisting of ten provinces and three territories. As the world's second largest country by total area, Canada's common border with the United States to the south and northwest is the longest in the world. The land that is now Canada was inhabited for millennia by various groups of Aboriginal peoples.

Canada is a federation that is governed as a parliamentary democracy and a constitutional monarchy with Queen Elizabeth II as its head of state. In 1867, Canada ceased being a British Colony and became the **Dominion of Canada.**

As a bilingual nation, both English and French are official languages at the federal level. One of the world's highly developed countries, Canada has a diversified economy that is reliant upon its abundant natural resources and upon trade—particularly with the United States. With the eighth-highest Human Development Index globally, the nation has one of the highest standards of living in the world.

Dancing is an intricate part of this. Dancing serves as a catalyst to socialization, an important aspect of individual and community development. Dances of native people in Canada are often connected with important rituals. Across Canada, there are many types of folk dance activities. Dancing is usually associated with an ethnic community, and often parents encourage children to participate in folk dance as a means of learning about and identifying with their cultural heritage.

Although documents that record the historical development of Canadian folk dance are scarce, some researchers believe that many dance forms grew from religious rituals. Each cultural area passed through its own evolution, although some areas have had more contact with external influences than others. In practice people invent, simplify and change steps, thereby creating variation on the original dance. Even many social dances enjoy a short, but intense popularity which then declines. Others, however, possess an unusual longevity, i.e., the waltz, polka, square dance and minuet of the 18th and 19th centuries are good examples.

Today, God is raising up a radical group of worshippers who will break

traditions of men to bring forth the new season of God's Kingdom. I have visited Canada only twice – my first trip there took place around 1997, and in 2010 with an apostolic team from Glory of Zion. God has people in that land who will not only govern in Canada, but in the nations of the earth. Pray for Canada. Although secular influences are increasing and bringing change to the society, declare that the influence of the gospel will increase. Pray for strong apostolic churches to be bold and strong to break down structures of the past and re-dig the wells of salvation in Canada. Also intercede for two people groups of Canada: The hundreds of thousands of First Nations people who are living in declining spiritual, physical, economic and social conditions and the Inuit Eskimos, whose way of life is daily compromised through growing social changes. Ask God's strong presence to visit them with His power and with the truth of the gospel.

Canada

Flag
Arms

Motto: *A Mari Usque Ad Mare* (Latin)
"From Sea to Sea"

Anthem: "O Canada" **Royal anthem:** "God Save the Queen"

Bahamas officially the Commonwealth of The Bahamas, is a country consisting of 29 islands, 661 cays, and 2,387 islets (rocks). The estimated population is 330,000. The capital is Nassau. The Original inhabitants were the Lucayans, a branch of the Arawakan-speaking Taino people.

Bahamian culture is a hybrid of African, Arawak Indian and European cultures. Though increasingly influenced by commercialization (due to tourism) and American culture, Bahamian culture retains much of its uniqueness, which is closely related to other creole cultures throughout the Caribbean.

Reportedly, most Bahamians adhere to Christianity. Religion is given the utmost importance within their society. Even the smallest village has a church. Bahamians are religiously enthusiastic and have high regard for education.

Traditional crafts include straw work on most islands (each one having a unique plaiting or braiding style) creating beautiful hats and baskets that are popular with many tourists, upon which their economy heavily depends. Storytelling and folklore played a large role in traditional entertainment in Bahamian communities. Many of these stories also carry wise lessons. Bahamian storytelling has witnessed some revival in recent years.

The most popular secular dance of The Bahamas is the Junkanoo (mentioned earlier in reference to Jamaica). This musical street masquerade is believed to be of West African origin and occurs in many towns across the Caribbean every December 26 and New Year's Day. The largest parade, Junkanoo, takes place in Nassau, the capital of the Bahamas.

Thousands of people dance through the streets wearing colorful costumes. The festival is an energetic parade accompanied with dancing to the rhythmic sounds of cowbells, drums and whistles.

Junkanoo is reminiscent of New Orleans' Mardi Gras and Rio de Janeiro's Carnival, but it is distinctly Bahamian and exists nowhere else. Junkanoo festivals reflect the culture of their individual island. The parade centers around a particular theme, which is reflected in their costumes, dance and music.

Let's thank God for their strong Christian heritage and let's pray and prophesy that the next generation will be strong in the Lord while holding true to the long standing Christian tradition of its people. Ask the Lord to empower the body of Christ in the Bahamas to remain faithful and focused, redeeming their secular traditions for the glory of God.

Commonwealth of The Bahamas

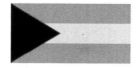

Flag
Coat of arms

Motto: "Forward, Upward, Onward, Together"

Royal anthem: "God Save the Queen"

Trinidad (Spanish: "Trinity") is the larger and more populous of the two major islands and numerous landforms which make up the islands of Trinidad and Tobago. It is the southernmost island in the Caribbean and lies just seven miles off the northeastern coast of Venezuela. It is also the fifth largest island in the West Indies.

Some of my most wonderful experiences have been in Trinidad. The people there are passionate worshippers with a heart to see the glory of the Lord fill their nation and the nations of the earth.

On one occasion, the ministry was truly powerful. God was bringing deliverance and healing to many. On the other hand, the bed I was sleeping in fell in...while I was in it! The water stopped so we took what is known as a Bottle Bath – taking showers using bottled water, and the ants ate my food! They had provided me a delicious dish called Roti. I could hardly wait to eat it, but I was not finished teaching my class. I asked them to place it in the microwave for me. I ran to the microwave upon completion of the class and found that the ants had a feast with my Roti! These experiences in no way reflect or represent the people or the culture of Trinidad, but it was a great learning experience. In Philippians 4:12, Paul said "I know both how to be abased (humbled), and I know how to abound: everywhere and in all things I am instructed both to be full and to be hungry, both to abound and to suffer need." Philippians 4:4 encourages us to "rejoice in the Lord always: and again I say, Rejoice." 1 Thessalonians 5:18 tells us to be thankful for all circumstances. This is what I did and I was humbled to be there.

Pray that Trinidad will be set at liberty – that they will love liberty and pursue liberty for the sake of the Kingdom of God.

Republic of Trinidad and Tobago

Flag
Coat of arms

Motto: "Together we aspire, together we achieve"

Anthem: Forged from the Love of Liberty

The **United States of America (United States, U.S., USA,** or **America)** is a federal constitutional republic comprising fifty states and a federal district. The country is situated mostly in central North America, where its forty-eight contiguous states and Washington, D.C., the capital district, lie between the Pacific and Atlantic Oceans. The state of Alaska is in the northwest of the continent and the state of Hawaii is located in the mid-Pacific. The country also possesses several territories in the Caribbean and Pacific.

At 3.79 million square miles and with over 308 million people, the United States is the third or fourth largest country by total area.

There is great variety in dance in the United States. Most recently, it has become the home of the hip hop dance and is a derivative of Rock and Roll and modern square dance. In fact, **nineteen U.S. states have designated square dancing as their official state dance.** The list of official state dances is a varied as the people, from the West Coast Swing to the Texas Two Step to the Polka and the Lindy Hop. The U.S. is also one of the major centers for modern dance.

The dances of Native-American <u>culture</u>, unlike some dances of our modern times, were tools for story-telling, not simply <u>exercise</u> or fun or movement for the sake of movement. The indigenous <u>cultures</u> of North America spent thousands of years embracing dance as a vital realization of life itself. The story of their history is still reflected in their dances today.

Native Americans mixed spirituality with their dances. It was a form of prayer, an expression of grief or joy, or a way for them to connect with nature. They honored everything from birth to marriage to death, healed sickness, or, in previous times, prepared for war. Even today, only dance may properly protect and send off a warrior to the modern-day military.

Dance has become the very embodiment of indigenous values and represents the response of Native Americans to complex and sometimes difficult historical experiences. It has been said of the Native

Americans..."Dance reflects the vast capacity of native peoples to endure culturally and to continue as a vital contemporary cultural phenomenon."

Early North Americans turned to dance as a tool for story-telling. Young men returning from battle or the hunt glowingly detailed accomplishments by "acting out" their experiences through dance. While there are many varieties indigenous to the Native American culture, I want to focus on only one.

The Native American Eagle dance performed by Indian tribes consists of movements that emulate an eagle. The dancers are clothed with replications of eagle attire. The performance includes sequences of songs and dances. In Native American tribes, the eagle has a symbolic meaning. These Native American tribes believe that the eagle has a spiritual connection to their prayers.

The Native American tribes performed the Eagle dance when there was a need for divine intervention. The Native Americans believe that the eagle symbolizes wisdom, strength and power. For the dancers, the eagle's feathers are sacred, especially the Golden Eagle and Bald Eagle. Therefore, it is a privilege to wear the eagle's feathers. Also, these Native American tribes believe that the eagle's feathers should never touch the ground. Moreover, the eagle's feathers are used as object decorations in the eagle dance ceremonies.

The performance of the Eagle dance is a depiction of the eagle's life cycle from birth to death. Two central dancers perform an imitation of the eagle's movements. Also, a group of male dancers provide background singing and drum music. However, there is no specific method to perform the dance. It varies with each tribe. In general, the dance consists of the eagle's day to day movements. For instance, the dancers may perform a replica of the animal's hunting and feeding progressions. The dancers make flapping movements to imitate the eagle's flight.

Different Indian tribes perform the Eagle dance during a sacred ceremony. The dance can be performed during any season, but it is normally performed in the early part of the spring season.

Pray for the United States. Pray for our leaders to fear God. Pray for our Christian legacy to be firm. Pray for the church of Jesus Christ to rise up without fear and stand for righteousness in the face of ungodly cultural, social and economic influences. Pray, prophesy, decree, declare and proclaim revival in this land! We are still "one nation under God." **Let us truly be a nation whose God is the Lord, trusting in Him and Him alone for our help!** And though we are a nation of many, may we become one and serve the one and only, true and living God.

United States of America

Flag
Great Seal

In God We Trust(official)
E Pluribus Unum (Latin: Out of Many, One)

Anthem: "The Star-Spangled Banner"

Puerto Rico (Spanish for "rich port") is made up of the main island of Puerto Rico and a number of smaller islands. The main island of Puerto Rico is the smallest by land area of the Greater Antilles. It, however, ranks third in population among that group of four islands, which also include Cuba, Hispaniola, and Jamaica.

Puerto Ricans often call the island Borinquen, from Borikén, its indigenous Taíno name, which means "Land of the Valiant Lord". The terms boricua and borincano derive from Borikén and Borinquen respectively, and are commonly used to identify someone of Puerto Rican heritage. The island is also popularly known in Spanish as "La Isla del Encanto" which means "The Island of Enchantment" in English.

The United States and Puerto Rico thus began a long-standing relationship. Puerto Rico is a commonwealth of the United States. This status provides local autonomy to the island and allows Puerto Rico to publicly display its flag. However, the government of Puerto Rico falls ultimately on the U.S. Congress although they carry local responsibility. The elected governor of Puerto Rico occupies the highest public office on the island.

I love to go to Puerto Rico to worship with the people there. Their love for the Lord and their passion to worship is contagious. As dancers, we work hard to develop choreography that will bless and minister to the Lord and His people. But God is the ultimate choreographer. I learned that in Puerto Rico. On one occasion during a worship service, the Lord sovereignly came in our midst. As we worshipped, it was as if God Himself choreographed what was to happen next. Hundreds of worshippers gathered without instruction from man, as if guided by a hand we could not see, into three perfect circles. An outer circle, inner circle and a third circle in the middle. As the **atmosphere shifter** in the service, I knew something was taking place in heaven that would change the nation. The presence of God descended and we worshipped for hours.

Puerto Rican dances are as diverse as its people. The plena, danza, sies, vals and bomba, as well as many folkloric dances, are part of the rich

Puerto Rican music/dance culture. Merengue, mambo and cha cha cha, make up a portion of the upbeat music and associated dances. Salsa is popular not just in the USA, but in many parts of the world.

The dancers of God in Puerto Rico are a strong community of worshippers who unite to change their nation. Our God is The Valiant Lord. Pray for God to show Himself mighty and strong on behalf of the people of Puerto Rico.

Commonwealth of Puerto Rico

Flag
Coat of arms

Motto:
Latin: Joannes Est Nomen Eius
Spanish: Juan es su nombre
English: John is his name

Anthem: La Borinqueña

Hawaii is the newest of the U.S. states (August 21, 1959), and is the only U.S. state made up entirely of islands. Because of its mid-Pacific location, Hawaii has many North American and Asian influences along with its own vibrant native culture. Its capital is Honolulu on the island of Oʻahu.

The aboriginal culture of Hawaii is Polynesian. Hula is the ancient dance of Hawaii. Although Hula began as a form of worship during religious ceremonies, it gradually evolved into a form of entertainment.

In Hula, every movement has a specific meaning. Even each expression of the dancer's hands has great significance. The movements of a dancer's body might represent certain plants, animals, or even war. Traditionally, it was not the dancer's hands, but the words that counted the most.

Hula is a religious dance, and the training of ancient hula dancers was quite strict. The students had to follow disciplined rules of conduct and had to obey their teachers in all things. For example, dancers could not cut their hair or nails and certain foods were forbidden. Hula continues to play a major role in the Hawaiian cultural revival which begun in the 1970's.

Today, the older style of Hula is performed in traditional costume to accompanying chanting and percussion only. The more modern style is accompanied by songs, ukuleles, guitars, and other instruments with dancers in colorful costumes.

During the 19th century, Hula dancing almost became extinct. The missionaries considered it to be ungodly and heathen. Today, there are hundreds of hula schools and less formal hula groups are active on every island and the mainland, teaching hula to thousands of students and keeping the old ways and traditional Hawaiian culture alive.

And because Hula was a religious dance, many Christians have redeemed their cultural dance by telling stories of God through Hula; however, not without controversy. Many ask, "how can you take a pagan form of worship, intended for the goddess Laka and Pele and "transform" it to the glory of Christ?"

State of Hawaii

Flag
Seal

Nickname(s) The Aloha State

Motto: "The Life of the Land is Perpetuated in Righteousness"
Anthem: "Hawaii's Own True Sons"

Psalm 67 sums up the message of the exhortation given to the nations of the earth – **to worship Him, to turn from idols to true faith in Him and to repent of trusting in anything or anyone other than Him.** Only then will any nation come to know the God of our salvation.

God be merciful unto us, and bless us;
and cause his face to shine upon us; Selah.
That thy way may be known upon earth,
thy saving health among all nations.
Let the people praise thee,
O God; let all the people praise thee.
O let the nations be glad and sing for joy:
for thou shalt judge the people righteously,
and govern the nations upon earth. Selah.
Let the people praise thee,
O God; let all the people praise thee.
Then shall the earth yield her increase;
and God, even our own God, shall bless us.
God shall bless us;
and all the ends of the earth shall fear him.

"Blessed is the nation whose God is the Lord"
Psalm 33:12

SECTION TWO

Chapter Five

SET FREE TO DANCE

Seeing yourself through His mirror.

Upon entering any dance studio, one of the first things you see is a mirror that covers most of the front wall, if not the entire wall. The purpose of this mirror is for you to look at yourself as you learn so you can see if anything is out of line or out of place. The premise is that if anything is out of line or out of place, you can change it and bring it into proper alignment!

Contrary to the popular belief of many dancers, the mirror is not there for us to admire ourselves or for us to see how wonderful we look in a leotard and tights! But I guess that is the problem. So many people in this world have self-esteem problems, so for them putting on leotards and tights are "too revealing." This is why people try to cover up with dance skirts, sweatshirts, T-shirts, sweat pants and anything else they can find. Many in the body of Christ have this mindset as well. They have learned to cover up things spiritually.

Many live this way daily - putting on anything that will help them feel better about themselves or that will keep people from knowing how bad they really feel about themselves. We hide the pain, the fear, the insecurity we feel inside just like we hide our bodies under layers of clothes in the dance studio.

Just put on a smile and everyone will think that we are okay. In the theater, we smile no matter what. The show must go on. We put on lots of make-up and fancy costume and for a brief period of time, we are someone else.

The mirror is indeed a direct reflection of how we look on the outside; it does not lie. But it is NOT who we are on the inside! Unfortunately, our society places too much emphasis on outward appearances. We are led to believe that if we are not a certain size, we are not good enough, not pretty enough, and/or not worthy enough.

In the Bible there is a story about a young man named David, who was out tending to his father's sheep when God sent Samuel, the prophet, to anoint him as the next King of Israel. At first all of David's brothers were considered as candidates for the position because they looked like a king outwardly. The Lord said to Samuel, "For the Lord does not see as man sees, for man looks at the outward appearance, but the Lord looks at the heart."

If I ask you to paint a self portrait of yourself, what would it look like? How do you see yourself? Do you see your failures or His victory? Do you see your weaknesses or His strength? Do you see your unrighteousness or do you know that you are the righteousness of God in Christ?

No matter how you see yourself, listen to what God says in Psalm 139:13-16:

> "You formed (weaved) my inward parts; You covered me in my mother's womb. I will praise You, for I am fearfully (this means to reverence – this means worship is in me) and wonderfully made. Marvelous (great and wonderful) are Your works (actions). And that my soul knows very well. My frame was not hidden from You. When I was made in secret, and skillfully wrought (embroidered) in the lowest part of the earth. Your eyes saw my substance, being yet unformed. And in your book they all are written. The days fashioned for me, when as yet there were none of them."

Precious child of God, He wants you to see yourself through His eyes, not through the eyes of the world or through the eyes of mirrors in a dance studio. **Let His Word become the mirror by which you see yourself.**

Let me tell you a story about Clara and Sarah. They were friends so Clara stood next to Sarah every Tuesday night at dance class. That was when the adult ballet class met. Sarah was petite and pretty and she seemed to be able to do all of the steps just right. But Clara was overweight and she had trouble catching on to most of the steps the teacher showed them. Clara often asked herself "now exactly why am I doing this?" Sarah encouraged Clara to take the class to help her lose some of the weight she had gained after childbirth. However, Clara began to find excuses to miss class. Any excuse would do, just as long as she did not have to stand next to Sarah and compare herself with her friend. When Sarah asked Clara why she had missed so many classes, she could not bring herself to tell her the truth. Eventually over time, she was able to share, "I think that you look pretty and I do not; therefore, it makes me feel bad about myself and I am not confident in who I am."

Many women have this same self image problem, whether it is with a friend in a dance class, with a family member or with a co-worker. And if not acknowledged, it will go unaddressed. Therefore, they come to accept it as part of life. They tell themselves, that is just the way it is, this is just who I am.

This is not meant to be a "feel good" chapter. It is meant to be an eye opening, truthful and liberating look into God's mirror so you can see who you really are and begin to say what God says about you. **You are not less than, you are more than a conqueror!** Jesus Christ did not die on the cross and rise on the third day for you to be in bondage to anything or anyone at anytime for any reason! No matter what life has presented you, FREEDOM is yours for the taking! Forgiveness is yours for the taking! Joy is yours for the taking! Peace is yours for the taking! Just ask and you shall receive from the heart of the ONE who created you and loves you so much that He sent His Son to die for you. Psalm 31:4 says, "Be strong and let your heart take courage, all you who hope in the LORD."

This chapter also has a learning assignment. **Take time to record onto a**

tape recorder Psalm 139:1-18, so you can HEAR God's Word being spoken over your life. Then, put your own movements to Psalm 139:1-18 and let this be a time of ministry to the Lord as His word ministers to you.

Memorize Psalm 139:13-18, so you can meditate on it day and night, no matter where you are or what you are doing. Get it in your spirit until it becomes real to you! Get it into your heart, so you will know who God has created you to be!

There is a lot in a name. It tells us who God has made us to be. For example in the Bible: Adam's name means red and ruddy, earth like, Eve means life-giver. Their names tell us who they were and how they functioned in God's plan for mankind. We read about Jacob and we see from his behavior that he lived up to his name, sub planter. But Jacob had a night where he wrestled with God (Genesis 32:22-32) and God changed his name to Israel, for He said, "Your name shall no longer be called Jacob, but Israel, for you have struggled with God and with men, and have prevailed."

This night impacted Jacob's life so tremendously that when he and his wife, Leah, starting having children, he recognized God giving them their names were extremely important.

Notice how God named each of Jacob's twelve sons: (Read Genesis, Chapters 29-30).
Reuben means seeing
Simeon means hearing
Levi means to be attached to
Judah means celebrated
Zebulun means habitation, to dwell with
Issachar means he will bring a reward
Dan means judged
Gad means a troop
Asher means happy
Naphtali means wrestling
Joseph means let him add
Benjamin means son of my right hand

As we read the story of Leah and Rachel in Genesis 29:31-35, we see that God opened the womb of Leah. She conceived and bore a son and she called his name Reuben. She said, "The Lord has looked upon my affliction. Now therefore, my husband will love me." She was hoping this would turn the heart of her husband to her, but his heart was still attached to Rachel.

Rachel was the daughter that Jacob thought he was marrying when he married Leah. You see, was tricked by his uncle into marrying another woman. In the Bible days when couples got married, the woman's face was cover, so you did not know who you were marrying until the honeymoon night.

This is what happened to Jacob. Instead of him getting Rachel as his wife, his uncle made a switch; therefore, he married Leah. Yes, Jacob was angry and disappointed, but he eventually accepted Leah as his wife.

As they knew each other intimately, they began having sons. One of the sons they had was name Simeon – "Because the Lord has heard that I am unloved, He has therefore given me this son also." The Bible says that Leah conceived again and bore another son, and she said, "Now this time my husband will become attached to me, because I have bore him three sons." She named him Levi. **There are times when we expect those closest to us to "see" us, "hear" us or be "attached" to us, but they are not.** It is at these times that we must look inside of ourselves to the ONE who lives inside of us and gave birth to Judah, just as Leah did. The Bible says that she conceived again and bore a son and said, "Now I will praise the LORD." She called his name Judah and stopped having children.

In barren moments in our lives or times of insecurity, we have to do as Leah did. We have to give birth to praise in these difficult situations, and let God become your praise. Let Him fill your with His purposes and let praises rise up to God -- from the deepest place in your heart and spirit cry out to God. Leah found her joy in praise and so can you. You are fearfully and wonderfully made. **REJOICE!**

Learn what your name means! My name, **Pamela, means loving one who is sweet as honey**. My middle name is Sue. **Sue means like a lilly or trumpet like.** My last name, **Hardy, means bold and robust!** So God said that I am a loving one who is sweet as honey who lifts up her voice like a trumpet with boldness! Know who God has created you to be and daily be conformed to the image of His dear Son! Rejoice means to jump for joy. May you jump for joy as you walk in the fullness of who God created you to be!

Pastor Maria taught me to begin my day with the Lord. One of the ways I encounter His presence is by having a time of worship unto the Lord. The New Testament word that we find most for worship is the Greek word Proskuneo. It means to prostrate yourself before God. It means to kiss toward the Master's hand as a dog licking the hand of his master. I have heard it said that we go higher by going lower. Once you have prepared a place to meet with God, lay prostrate before Him. Go low, not only in the position of your body, but in the position of your heart. This is how you turn your heart upward. This is first position.

Prostration speaks of humility before a Holy God. We must humble ourselves before God daily. We must prepare our bodies for His holy habitation. For even Jesus humbled Himself and became obedient unto death, even the death of the cross. So let this same mind be in us - a mind that says "God, here I am to worship you. I am totally submitted to you. I give you my life. I humble myself before you. Take complete control of my life. I lay it before you."

I encourage you to stop where you are now and lay prostrate before God. Stretch your arms out to the side. This will position your body to the shape of a cross. For our Lord admonishes us to take up our cross daily. Luke 9:23 says, "...If anyone desires to come after Me, let him deny himself, and take up his cross daily, and follow Me."

Galatians 6:14 says, "But God forbid that I should boast except in the cross of our Lord Jesus Christ, by whom the world has been crucified to me, and I to the world." Let us not boast in a perfect turn out, let us not boast in flawless technical skills, but let us boast in the cross of Christ with a heart that is turned upward to Him. Whatever we consider as gain let it be counted as loss for Christ."

On the third day, He arose with all power in His hands. So we, too, can rise from a position of prostration, humility and complete submission to God to walk in His love. We can run in His power and not get weary. We can dance into His freedom!

As you rise, take time to minister unto the Lord with a spontaneous song or dance. A spontaneous dance is one that flows from your heart to God. There is no right or wrong as long as you are expressing to God the love and thanksgiving that is in your heart. God created us all different. No two people are exactly the same. Even twins have different DNA. I believe that God has songs, music, books and even dances from His heart and throne that He is just waiting to release into the earth through each one of us. Your expression of worship from your heart to God is like no other, and you alone bring a pleasing fragrance to Him that no one else can bring. You do not have to be concerned about what other people think, so BE FREE! REJOICE!

I do not believe that before David danced before the Lord, he said, "Wait God, let me go take a dance class and when my technique is perfect, I will dance before you." No! He expressed his thankfulness to God with all that was in him. When we look at the Hebrew words found in 1 Chronicles 15:29 that describe David's dance, we see that he was **leaping and stamping wildly** for joy as if the limbs of His body were going to be separated! WOW! That is what I call total abandonment unto God! He was truly set free to worship!

Let your first position (heels touching) be you touching God with a heart turned upward as you dance before the King.

I love the words to a popular worship song I often sing....
"This is my desire, to honor you, Lord with all my heart, I worship you. All I have within me I give you praise, all that I adore is in you. Lord I give you my heart, I give you my soul. I love for you alone. Every breath that I take, every moment I'm awake, Lord have your way in me."

During your time with the Lord, also have your Bible, a notepad, a pen and study Bibles. This will help to prepare you to hear from God, prepare your heart to obey the Lord and allows Him to order your day.

Psalm 139:17-18 reads, "How precious also are Your thoughts to me, O God! How great is the sum of them! If I should count them, they would be more in number than the sand; When I awake, I am still with You."

Don't you want to begin your day knowing what God's thoughts are toward you for that day? Quiet your spirit, meditate on His word, and let your first position be the upward turning of your heart toward God. To meditate means to mutter, to meditate or to speak. God told Joshua to meditate (Joshua 1:8) day and night in His word, in order to observe to do according to all that God had told him. For then he would make his way prosperous and then he would have good success. The same applies to us today. When we meditate on the Word of God daily, then God will make our way prosperous and we will have good success.

John 8:31-32, 36 (King James Version) says, "Then said Jesus to those Jews which believed on him, If ye continue in my word, then are ye my disciples indeed; And ye shall know the truth, and the truth shall make you free.
If the Son therefore shall make you free, ye shall be free indeed."

Shout FREEDOM! Now REJOICE!

Chapter Six

SPIRITUAL REQUIREMENTS FOR THE MINISTER OF DANCE

In preparing yourself for the ministry of dance, we must realize that our first call is to Jesus Himself. We are called first to draw closer to Him. We must seek to know Him, His face, and His heart. Therefore our dance ministry will become a result of the overflow of having spent time with Him. It is when we activate these requirements that then and only then can we truly answer the call to ministry. He must always be our first love.

The Scriptures tell us that God is seeking worshippers, not dancers (See John 4:23-24). Although ability is necessary, the Scripture does not exhort us to "praise Him in the dance if you have been to ballet class." Those who will worship in Spirit and in truth are those who God calls.

Because there is no scriptural reference that tells us to "sit and watch while others dance," our dance must truly be a priestly ministry, bringing Christ to the people, and/or the people to Christ. We are never to be the focus. **Because dance is such a visible ministry, it is imperative for us to endeavor to lay self on the altar and seek to "BE YE HOLY, FOR I AM HOLY" (1 Peter 1:16).**

God wants us to make time to meet with Him daily -- for He desires to meet with us. Let us desire to spend time with God until our dances come from Him. We need dances that are Spirit to spirit: Dances that will bring change in the lives of others. God has dances from His heart and throne that He wants to pour out through us. Therefore, we must learn to be visual demonstrations of what God is saying and doing in the Sprit. We minister His messages, not our own. We must empty our own dances and make room for His. We must learn to express the truths of God's heart. *Dance ministry is NOT for entertainment.*

We must become transparent in our worship. There are no short cuts. We must allow God to break us in worship so we can begin to learn true expression. Let's yearn for that which is authentic. You cannot fake the anointing. The anointing is not just for your gift – it is for your whole life. Ministry must come from the overflow.

Worshippers who are consumed with a fiery passion for Jesus will win the end-time harvest. The ultimate in our worship is not the expression of the worship - but rather the knowledge of His presence. We are called to protect the presence of the Lord, both in our personal lives and in our corporate gatherings. Let's not reduce our expressions of worship to mere fleshly activities. His presence and His anointing are the only things that validate our expressions of worship, not our skill or expressive ability. Let's learn to hear from God – learn to know what the Spirit is saying to the church.

I challenge you to begin your day with God. If you do not already have a daily time set aside for seeking His face, make it a priority to begin immediately. Each morning, rise earlier than normal, go into your prayer closet – a place where there will be no distractions. Have a time of worship, Bible study and prayer. **It is vital for the worshipper to minister TO God before ministering FOR God.** Then, and only then will we truly be vessels prepared for the Master's use.

Five Positions of the Feet and Legs:

Before we look at the "why" of dance as ministry, let's look at the five positions of the feet and legs learned in a ballet class. In Chapter 1, we discussed first position, but in each of the five positions, the dancer stands with the legs turned out from the hip sockets. This causes the toes to be turned outward, facing away from each other. *I look at this as if I am looking outward to see the needs of others.* As we allow the Lord to order our steps, He will lead us and guide us into all truth and teach us how to effectively serve others.

The Bible tells us to "Praise Him in the dance" in Psalm 149:3 and Psalm 150:4. It does not say to praise Him in the dance only if you have taken ballet classes! Ballet is not a pre-requisite for dancing before or for the Lord. Yes, the study of ballet can certainly help you to develop proper body placement, but we are all call to dance before the Lord whether we are trained dancers or not. This is what the Lord taught me and I want to share this insight with His body.

Taking ballet or any other dance classes are commendable, and you will gain a great foundation from which to build a solid and clear movement vocabulary, thus enabling you to be an effective messenger of God's Word through movement. So if you decide to take dance classes, take them "WITH" the Lord. As you take classes, let the Word be the basis for each movement. Concentrate on the truths of God's Word as you are dancing, as much as the guidance you are receiving from your instructor.

Here is an example:

When the dancer stands in **first position**, the heels are together, touching one another but the toes are facing outward. I look at this as me touching God while looking outward to the needs of those around me.

When the dancer stands in **second position**, the legs are slightly apart. One must be centered and balanced as we must be centered and balanced in the Lord. The weight must be evenly distributed.

When the dancer stands in **third position**, the heel of one foot comes half way across the other foot, meeting in the center at the arch of the foot. It is one of the easiest positions and is one of the first positions taught to children. Perhaps, we must be reminded to come to Him as little children. It also helps to maintain the balance of the dancer. Even so we must be sure that we are daily maintaining our balance in the Lord, so that the enemy will not be able to throw us off center.

When the dancer stands in **fourth position**, the feet are placed apart, one in front of the other, in such a way that the heel of the front foot is in line with the heel of the back foot. The legs are turned out from the hip sockets, thus the feet are facing opposite directions. In the closed fourth, the feet are placed apart, with the heel of the front foot directly in front of the toe of the back foot. Either way, this speaks to us again of balance. The weight must always be evenly distributed between both legs. Your body must not be placed too far forward or too far back. As we stand strong in the Lord, we must not be too far forward. This represents a proud and haughty spirit. We must not be too far back. God did not call us to shrink back in shame or fear. Bottom line: Let's not run ahead of God and let's not fear to follow after Him. Stand strong in the Lord.

When the dancer stands in **fifth position**, one foot is hidden directly behind the other foot, which represents the fact that we must be hidden in Him. From the front, it gives the appearance of one foot. We must be one with Him, so that He is the only One the world sees.

Here are some other terms used in ballet and how they relate to the Word of God.

- No dancer can dance without using their Plie. Plie means to bend. I believe this means that we must be willing to bend – to yield -- to be pliable in His hands. Trying to dance with straight, stiff legs cannot be done! We must not be stiff-necked and unyielding, but we must be willing to bend our will to conform to His.

- A dancer must also learn to properly releve. Releve means to rise! He is calling us all to daily rise to new levels in Him. When we rise, we see from His perspective!

- Passe means to pass. We are to leave the old behind and pass over into the new that God has for us! For it is written in 1 John 3:14, "We have passed from death to life..."

- Frappe means to strike! With the authority we have been given, we strike the enemy! Psalm 18:40 says, we have been given the neck of our enemies.

- Degage means to disengage. Let's disengage from everything that is not of God! Colossians 3 admonishes us that since we have been risen with Christ, let us seek those things that are above. Let us set our affections on things that are above, not on things on the earth. We are dead to the things of this world and our lives are hidden with Christ in God.

- Port de Bras means carriage of the arms. Let us remember that He has redeemed us with His outstretched arms. Therefore, we can ask the Lord to allow the carriage of our arms to be an extension of His grace and mercy reaching out to help redeem others!

- Tendu means stretched. Although it is a movement of the feet, God stretched out His hand and performed miracles for His children. I hear the Lord saying, "stretch yourself out on me and watch the miracles I will do for you!" Ask Him to allow miracles to come forth as we stretch ourselves to manifest His glory!

- Glissade means to glide. May He cause our feet to be like hinds feet so we can "glide" upon the high places!

- Derrier means back! Do NOT go back – look back – think back! We are meant to always move forward!

- Epaulment means shouldered. Isaiah 9:6-7 tells us that when Jesus came, He brought a government on His shoulders - for us! "And of the increase of His government and peace, there will be no end!"

- Attitude is a position of the leg. As Dr. Myles Munroe (one of God's 21st century generals in leadership training) says, "An attitude of gratitude will change your altitude. It will take you higher in His presence." Let's make sure our attitudes are rightly aligned.

- Develope means to develop. God wants us to be fully developed, not mere children tossed to and fro by every wind of doctrine, but He wants us to grow up and mature in Him so we can reflect Him in all things.

- Battement means beating. It can be a repetitious movement and to be done correctly over and over while still maintaining proper balance and alignment takes practice and discipline. 1 Corinthians 9 says that as we strive to obtain the imperishable crown, we must discipline our bodies. Let us not be as those who "beat the air."

- Grand Jete is a big throw. Let's rejoice that we can throw or cast all of our cares upon the Lord because He cares for us!

- Assemble means to assemble – to bring together. Let us not forsake the assembling of ourselves as the scripture admonishes us in Hebrews 10:25 but let us "encourage one another...as we see the "Day" approaching," for our God is faithful!

As a practical application, take a ballet class or take time to go through the ballet portion of the Set Free To Dance DVD. As you go through each exercise, allow the Word applications above to saturate your mind. Meditate on the Scriptures so that as you are working through each ballet exercise, you will remember the spiritual applications. **Take class with the Lord and allow His Word to work in your life.**

Determine to be a prepared vessel, willing to protect the presence of the Lord through daily discipline in worship. Let a new level of passion arise in your heart to take you to a place in worship unto our King.

Chapter Seven

WHY DANCE MINISTRY?

As I mentioned earlier, the Lord met me and told me He would take me around the world to dance for Him. That tells me that **dance ministry is important to God.** As I began to seek the Lord and to study His Word, I learned that the Bible has quite a bit to say about dance! I began to ask questions. Is dance really significant in the church today? Why are we seeing such a worldwide restoration of dance in the body of Christ? Is it just the latest thing to do?

I believe the answer to all these questions can be found in Jeremiah 31:13, which tells us that in the last days, the virgin shall rejoice in the dance, both young men and old together. God Himself will turn mourning to joy and bring His comfort. Rejoicing will replace sorrow.

I believe that we are indeed living in the last days. The word *virgin* in that scripture translates in the original text as the word *bride*. Therefore, it can be read as follows: "In the last days, the bride shall rejoice in the dance." It is not just the latest thing to do just because the church across town has a dance ministry. Dance in the church is a fulfillment of prophecy. In these last days, we see God rebuilding and restoring His church. I believe that God wants us to realize that we are part of something that is so much bigger than we are. As I travel to other countries, I see that God is working the same way throughout the body of Christ.

In the dictionary, dance is described as emotional movements of the body: to whirl, to spin, to leap, to jump, to extend the hands, to stamp the feet. The dance a part from God is merely exercise. **To the child of God, dance is an outward expression of an inward relationship, born out of a heart that desires to offer praise and worship to the Creator.** Isaiah 43:7 tells us that we were made to glorify Him - to express back to Him our appreciation of His worth. Dance is not the culprit. It is the motive of the heart. Acts 17:28 says, "...in Him we live and move and have our being."

Amos 9:11-12 corresponds with Acts 15:16. Both scriptures speak about the restoration of the Tabernacle of David. The Tabernacle of David was where worship was first set in order. In David's Tabernacle (see I Chronicles 15-16), we see many expressions of worship:

The ministry of **singing and singers**	1 Chronicles 15:16-27
The ministry of **musicians with instruments**	1 Chronicles 23:5
The ministry of the **Levites before the Ark**	1 Chronicles 16:4, 6
The ministry of the **scribe**	1 Chronicles 18:16
The ministry of **thanking the Lord**	1 Chronicles 16:4
The ministry of **praise**	1 Chronicles 16:4
The ministry of **Psalms**	1 Chronicles 16:9
The ministry of **rejoicing and joy**	1 Chronicles 16:10
The ministry of **clapping hands**	Psalm 47:1
The ministry of **shouting**	1 Chronicles 15:28
The ministry of **dancing**	1 Chronicles 15:29
The ministry of **lifting the hands**	Psalm 141:2
The ministry of **worship**	1 Chronicles 16:29
The ministry of **seeking the Lord**	1 Chronicles 16:10-11
The ministry of **spiritual sacrifices**	Psalm 27:6
The ministry of **saying Amen!**	1 Chronicles 16:36

Acts 15:16 says...
> After this I will return
> And will build the Tabernacle of David which has fallen down;
> I will rebuild its ruins,
> And I will set it up.

Then in verse 17 it tells us why God is restoring the Tabernacle – *"so that the residue of men might seek after the Lord."* So part of the purpose for the restoration of our expressions of worship is to cause people to want to know Him. Therefore, we must begin to look beyond the expression of dance to the Spirit behind the expression. Let us lead people beyond the dance to the Lord of the Dance.

There is no place in the Word of God that says sit down and watch people dance. That is why we must study, know and understand the Word and take our places as New Testament priests. Our call is to lead the people to God who alone can meet their needs. We must hear God and tell the people what God is saying. We must dance messages of God's love, God's healing and God's peace. We are not just dancers. We are ministers of the Gospel, called to be atmosphere shifters. Therefore, we must dance God's Word.

The one time in scripture dance was watched as entertainment, was in the case of Herodias' daughter. As she danced before King Herod (see Mark 6:14-29), the Bible says her dance "pleased" the King so much that he allowed her to ask for whatever she wanted. She asked for the head of John the Baptist. If our lives and our dances of worship and praise please THE KING, we can ask what we will. What shall we ask for? Most of us would ask for something for ourselves: "Lord, please anoint ME; Lord, help ME not to forget the steps; or Lord, help ME not to trip and fall or run into anyone else!" We should be asking for God to release His Spirit into the hearts and lives of those who God has sent us to minister to. Ask for souls. Pray for His Spirit to release those present into a new place of worship. Ask for deliverance to take place - for healing to take place - for His joy and peace to be released.

When you see dance mentioned in the Word of God, it was often congregational. Since every people group has dances that are indigenous to their culture, dance was a part of their community life. Everyone danced - the men, the women and the children. Dance was a part of everyday life. It is recorded that dances were done at harvest time. Dance was a part of weddings, worship and warfare.

In Israel, there were three main events associated with dancing:

THE HARVEST - Matthew 9:37-38 says, "....The harvest truly is plentiful, but the laborers are few. Therefore pray the Lord of the harvest to send out laborers into His harvest." We are living in the time of the end time harvest. Even as they danced for a natural harvest, we can dance for a spiritual harvest.

THE FEAST OF TABERNACLES - The Feast of His coming. As His return gets closer, we will see an increase in dancing. Exodus 15:20 tells of the miraculous deliverance of the children of Israel from many years in bondage to Pharaoh. God brought them through the Red Sea, which represents the fact that we have been delivered from death, hell, sin, sickness and the grave itself and we have been brought through the blood of Jesus Christ. The Bible says Miriam, the Prophetess, led all the women in the dance. It was significant that she was the one who led in the dance. It was a custom in those days for the female relative of the deliverer to go out to meet and greet the returning victor after the battle. Who was the deliverer? Moses. Miriam was his sister. Who is our deliver? Who is our returning Victor? JESUS! WE are His relative, His betrothed and the closer His return gets, the more we will see an increase in dance in the body of Christ.

TIMES OF MARRIAGE - Revelation 19:7 says let us rejoice and be glad for the marriage supper of the lamb has come and the bride has made herself ready! Our dances are dances of Victory and our dances say to God, we know that you are our Victor and we celebrate your victory. Our dances say to each other, this is who our God is! Be encouraged! We have the Victory! Our dances say to the world, "Come, taste and see that our God is good and in Him, you can have victory." Our dance says to our enemies, "Your time is short and we dance on the necks of all our enemies with dances of victory" (Psalm 18:40).

Tabernacle ministry listings in this chapter were taken from *Dancing Before the Lord* by Marilyn Wright.

Chapter Eight

ARE YOU CALLED?

Our first call is to worship. The Bible does not say that the Lord seeks dancers. John 4:23-24 does say that the Lord seeks people to WORSHIP Him. Proverbs 8:34 says, "Blessed is the man whom I find watching DAILY at my gates." **We should not have a public ministry unless we have a private one.** That requires daily time spent in the presence of God. We must be those who would spend time with God, and then go forth to dance, to sing, to demonstrate those things we have heard while in His presence. We must learn to be visual demonstrations of what God is saying and doing. Romans 12:1-2 admonishes us to present our bodies, all of our selves to the Lord as living sacrifices. I believe that God has dances from His heart - dances from Heaven that we have not experienced yet. I believe that there are dances that He wants to release into the earth through His church. These are dances that will bring changes in the lives of others -- dances that are demonstrated with the body, but originated in the Spirit first. We must minister Spirit to spirit, not flesh to flesh.

Examine your heart and be honest as you allow the Holy Spirit to search your heart. Then ask yourself these questions:
1. God did YOU call me to dance ministry or did I call myself?
2. Am I dancing just because I like to dance or because I saw someone else dance and I made the decision to move forward?
3. Why am I doing this? Am I only dancing because my pastor asked me to or because I received a word from a prophet?

4. What are my expectations and what are those expectations based on?
5. Have I truly consecrated my life and the gift of dance to the Lordship of Jesus Christ?
6. God, how am I to dance?
7. When am I to dance?
8. Where am I to dance?
9. What kind of dances do you want me to do? Shall I work with the children? Shall I use dance as outreach beyond the walls of the church? Are you calling me to take your dances to the prisons or to nursing homes?
10. Do you want me to take technique classes?

Once you have settled these questions in your heart and established a disciplined, daily time with God, we must then lay a foundation in the Word of God. If you believe God has called you to the ministry of dance, it is imperative that you know as much as you can about the ministry you say God has called you to.

What are some areas of dance we see in the church?

Dances of praise can be described as those dances directed to God for what He has done. The word we see for praise in Psalm 149:3 and Psalm 150:4, comes from the root word Halal, which is where we get the word Hallelujah. It means to shine, to boast, to act clamorously foolish before God. It means to celebrate Jesus! These dances are characterized with movements of jumping, spinning and leaping. It may include faster, more joyful movements. Ask the Lord if He is calling you to do dances of praise in the midst of the congregation.

Spontaneous dances are those dances that are not choreographed. Those dances that come from the Holy Spirit or those dances that come from our heart that we express to God. Are you comfortable with spontaneous dances or do you need everything to be choreographed? Do you need someone else to give you specific movements to do? Are you free to move as Holy Spirit leads you?

Dances of celebration can be seen in Exodus 15:20. We read that God did a miracle and delivered the children of Israel from many years in bondage to Pharaoh. He brought them through the Red Sea, which represents the fact that we have been delivered from death, sin, sickness and the grave itself as stated earlier. We have been bought through the blood of Jesus. The Scripture tells us that Miriam, the Prophetess, led all the women in the dance. Everyone danced and celebrated after seeing God destroy their enemies! This what Jesus has done for us. He has conquered our enemies! Jesus is our deliverer, our victor. Let's celebrate with dancing! We welcome His soon return with dances that celebrate His victory. Do you truly celebrate in the dance because you know that you have been delivered from darkness into His marvelous light?

Dances of worship have to do with who God is. In the Old Testament, the Hebrew word *shachah* means to press down, to prostrate, to pay homage to royalty. The Hebrew word *Barak* means to kneel down and to bless God as an act of Adoration. The New Testament word used most for worship is the Greek word *Proskuneo*. It means to prostrate yourself, to kiss toward the master's hand, as a dog would worship His master. Are you worshipping in Spirit and truth before God or are you performing for people?

Prophetic dance comes from the Heart of God to edify, exhort and comfort. For more, see the chapter on Prophetic dance.

Israeli dances were community dances. These dances were done as circle dances. Everyone participated. They were community dances, and sometimes they were done around an altar to celebrate the goodness of God. Are you comfortable leading others in dances of celebration?

At times, the word *dance* translates as travail. These dances of intercession can mirror labor and travail of childbirth in the natural. As things are birthed in the natural, so we may labor by unction of the Holy Spirit. Things can be birthed by the Spirit of God, in the realm of the Spirit, and then be manifested in the natural. God may choose to use dance to birth His purposes in the earth. These can also include dances of intercession. Have you ever given birth through dance in the spirit realm?

As well, Warfare dance can include dances of intercession. God has called us to be His authority in the earth. Warfare dances are characterized with strong movements of the hands and feet. Romans 6:13 says, we yield our members as instruments of righteousness. The word *instruments* can be translated as weapons. It could read, we yield our members (body) as weapons of righteousness. Are you able to do a warfare dance because you know God has given us the victory?

What is the function of dance in the body of Christ today?

There are several purposes and different ways that dance can function in the church. I have listed a few of them below.

1. **To establish His Kingdom:** One of the ways we go forth to establish the Kingdom of God in the earth is through the authority in our feet. Feet symbolize dominion, rulership and authority. What God said to Joshua, He says to us. Joshua 1:3 tells us that every piece of ground our feet tread upon He has given to us. Psalm 18:40 tells us that He has given us the necks of our enemies. Luke 10:19 says, we tread upon (trample under foot) serpents, scorpions and all the power of the enemy and nothing shall harm us. Malachi 4:2-3 says, God will make our enemy as ashes under the souls of our feet.

Feet can bring deliverance with stamping of the feet. We reclaim the territory with our feet and lead the people of God into God's victory. As we lead others into God's presence, we are filled with His glory. Then, we take that glory to the world. His glory shall cover the earth as we go forth to establish His Kingdom.

2. **To Express joy in victory and to lead others into praise unto God:** Even as Miriam, the Prophetess, led the women in the dance, it was an expression of joy for the victory God had brought to His people.

We are to express that joy because of the victory Jesus won for us. We are not "just dancers," we are worship leaders even as Miriam was. We lead people into the presence of God and ultimately, into His victory.

3. **To rejoice in the Lord and to usher in His presence:** In 2 Samuel 6: 14-16 and 1 Chronicles 15, we read about David. During the reign of King Saul, he had not sought to bring the ark to God's people. The ark represented the presence of God in the midst of His people. As David sought to bring the ark back, the word tells us that he danced before the Lord with all of His might! The King was leaping and stamping wildly for joy. He was willing to look foolish in the eyes of others in order to express his thankfulness to God. His wife, Michal, did not like the way David expressed himself to God and because of this, she was barren. We must be careful how we judge others when they do things for the Lord that we may not fully understand.

4. **We are given permission to praise God in the dance in Psalm 149:3 and Psalm 150:4.** In these scriptures, it shows us that dance is one of the ways that we should praise our God. The word *dance* in these scriptures denotes a round dance, sometimes done around an altar, and other times at feasts when the brethren were rejoicing together. Thus, the purpose would be to celebrate the Lord as corporate worshippers gathered together. On one of our trips to Israel, we saw this word in action. We went to the Western Wall at the beginning of Shabat. As we were approaching the wall, we could hear the songs and the dances. Yes, we could hear the dancing! There was such an excitement in the air that it engaged our hearts and our spirits. Once we arrived, we saw many Jewish men dancing and celebrating the Lord in the round dance. They sang as they danced with their children on their shoulders. In the middle of their circle were groups of women and children dancing. I stood in amazement at what I was seeing. My heart was filled with so much joy. They then danced down to the Wall and had a time of prayer to God. After their time of prayer, they go home for food and fellowship. Let's pray that the spirit of dancing and rejoicing in the goodness of our God will break out in every heart, in every church, in every home, and in every nation!

5. **Through dance we can bring healing, liberty and deliverance.** Isaiah 58:6 speaks of loosing the "bands of wickedness." The word *loose* is the Hebrew word Nathar and it means to shake, to let loose, to untie. You may have seen people in worship services shaking their hands or their bodies or turning in circles. These are movements that can bring liberty and deliverance, which can release healing in the body, soul or spirit.

<u>What does God's Word say about dance as it relates to praise and worship?</u>

There are words that depict movement and give purpose to our dance.

1. The book of Exodus reveals to us the story of the Passover and tells us how God delivered His children from many years in bondage to Pharaoh. God told them to take a lamb without blemish, kill the lamb, take some of the blood and put it on two doorposts and on the lintel of their houses. He said in Exodus 12:13, "And when I see the blood, I will pass over you; and the plague shall not be on you to destroy you...." *Passover* is the Hebrew word *Pasach* and it means to Passover as in leaping. Let us leap for joy because the death angel passes over us!

2. Psalm 5:11 says, "But let all those rejoice who put their trust in You..." The word *rejoice* is an action word that means to jump for joy. Psalm 108:3 says, "I will praise You O Lord, among the peoples..." The word *praise* here means to praise the Lord with extended hands and graceful gestures. Sometimes praise has a plurality attached to the word, meaning a lot of extended hands praising and worshipping God through movements.

3. Zephaniah 3:17 says, that God is rejoicing over us with gladness. The word *rejoicing* there is the word giyl or guwl in Hebrew, and it implies that Jesus rejoices over us with spinning, under the influence of a violent emotion. He loves us so much and He is jealous over us. Therefore, He rejoices over us. Let us also spin and rejoice in His presence and because of His goodness. We love Him because He first loved us.

4. John chapter 4 tells the story of the woman at the well and her encounter with the King. This is a very familiar story in the church and many preachers preach about it. When preached on often the focus will be on verse 24, "God is Spirit, and those who worship him must worship him in spirit and truth." However, I want us to look at verses 7-14 when Jesus asked the Samaritan woman to give Him a drink. He then said to her, "If you knew the gift of God, and who it is who says to you, "Give me a drink," you would have asked Him, and He would have given you living water." He goes on to say, "...whoever drinks of the water that I shall give him will never thirst. But the water that I shall give him will become in him a fountain of water springing up into everlasting life." So if our spirits are springing up and leaping for joy, why should our physical bodies not do the same?

5. Colossians 2:15 tells us that Jesus made a public spectacle of principalities and powers, "triumphing" over them. The word *triumph* is a Greek word that means a clamatorial procession or a march of war and victory. In other words, Jesus triumphed over the enemy and He marched to victory. We, too, can march and declare the victory our God has won for us!

Practical application: Look at the last five scripture passages and then practice each one of them.

- Begin by leaping for joy because the death angel has passed over you.
- Then rejoice in the Lord! Jump for joy! And again I say, rejoice! Jump for joy! Then extend your hands and begin to worship Him with graceful gestures.
- Begin to reflect on the goodness of the Lord and let your heart be filled with His love. Spin around and thank Him for loving you then tell Him how much you love Him because He first loved you. He has loved us with an everlasting love and with His loving-kindness He draws us. His banner over us is love (Song of Solomon 2:4).
- Receive from the fountain of living waters. Let your spirit, soul and body rejoice; jump for joy.

- Then do a victory march to declare that God has triumphed over your enemies!

Make full proof of your calling. **Go forth to lead and encourage others to worship the true and living God. He alone is worthy!**

Chapter Nine

STARTING A DANCE MINISTRY IN YOUR CHURCH

When we have experienced God in worship, we want to lead others to do the same. Starting a dance ministry in your church can be a great way to help facilitate this worship experience. The place to start is to ask yourself how dance can best serve the body of Christ of which you are a part of. As you pray about beginning a dance ministry in your church, there are several factors to consider.

First of all, dance ministry must be a vision and goal of your Pastor. You must know the vision of your church, and how dance ministry can best serve that vision:
- Will dance be a part of praise and worship or only during "special" ministry times?
- Will the dance ministry consist of children, teens and/or adults?
- Do you have a clear vision and purpose for the ministry?
- Who are you accountable to?
- What scripture is the ministry based on?
- Are there men interested in being a part of the dance ministry?
- How often will the dance ministry meet?
- What are the rules and regulations of the ministry?
- What else is required to be a part of the ministry?
- What ages will be included?

These are some of the questions that must be clear before you begin.

Do not despise small beginnings. It is better to have two or three members of the dance ministry who are called and truly have a heart to worship and work in unity than to have a larger group who may not be completely worship focused. Unity is a must.

Submission to leadership and willingness to work as a group is a necessity. There should be regular input from the leadership in the church. Be open to receive advice and constructive criticism (if needed) from your leadership. Keep communications open.

The dance ministry should be part of the praise and worship team. The dancers should never be a separate group with no connection to the rest of the body.

Also, it is best to instruct and educate the congregation so they will understand what role the dancers will have in the services and how they are there to serve at the church.

Select a dance leader who clearly knows the vision, mission and purpose dance is to serve in your local body. The leader must be one with good leadership skills, one who can establish goals, be a clear communicator and be able to accurately and spiritually discern where the ministry is. In addition, the leader must know how to make the ministry grow and how to confer with church leaders. Also, the leader must be one who can be led by Holy Spirit - one who does not dominate or manipulate whereby others will be able to submit to his/her authority and leadership.

Once a leader or leaders have been established, ask God how to make the ministry grow. Some churches feel led to hold auditions in an effort to maintain a certain level of excellence in skill, and other churches have a "whosoever will, let them come" policy. Whichever you feel is best for your church, I suggest that you focus on the call, more than the skill. Set standards for your ministry. As stated earlier, how often will you meet? Will there be consequences for being late or for missing rehearsals? **Remain consistent once the standards are set.**

During your weekly meetings, it is important to take time to pray, to worship, to study the Word of God before you begin working on your choreography. Always put the Lord first and He will honor your efforts.

Laying a foundation in the Word is a must. You need a solid foundation upon which to build.

Let's look at some **Old Testament Hebrew Words** for dance:

Mechowlah (4246) - a dance: Reference Exodus 15:20

Chagag (2287) - to move in a circle, to observe a festival: Reference Exodus 23:14

Karar (3769) - to dance, to whirl about: Reference II Samuel 6:14

Dalag (1801) - to spring: Reference II Samuel 22:30

Halijkah(1979) - walking in a procession, to march: Reference Psalm 68:24

Yahah (3034) - to worship with extended hands: Reference Psalm 92:1

Towdah (8426) - to extend the hands in adoration, a choir of worshippers: Reference Psalm 95:2

Barak (1288) - to kneel, to bless God as an act of adoration: Reference Psalm 95:6

Shachah (7812) - to prostrate in worship to God: Reference Psalm 96:9

Raqad (7540) - to stamp, to spring about wildly for joy: Reference Psalm 114:4,6

Machowl (4234) - a round dance: Reference Psalm 1493; Psalm 150:4

New Testament Greek Words

Orcheomai (3738) - to dance in a rank or regular motion: Reference Matthew 11:17

Skirtao (4640) - to jump: Reference Luke 6:23

Choros (5525) - a round dance: Reference Luke 15:25

Hallomai (242) - to jump, to gush as a fountain: Reference John 4:14

Proskuneo (4352) - to prostrate oneself in homage: Reference John 4:20-24

Exallomai (1814) - to leap, to spring forth: Reference Acts 3:8
Agalliao (21) - to jump for joy, to leap: Reference Revelation 19:7

Dance ministry must draw focus to the Lord and the Word, not the person or works of the dancer. We want to show forth the glory of His praise. For that reason, dance ministry requires:

1. A heart fully yielded to the Lord Jesus Christ
   - A. Worship that comes forth from a true love relationship with Jesus
   - B. Ministry TO God before ministry FOR God
   - C. Quality time in the Word and prayer
   - D. A holy life, a pure heart, pure motives
2. Calling - a time of preparation to prove your calling
   - A. We must dance with the anointing that will destroy the yokes of bondage
   - B. Dance from a heart of worship, not entertainment
   - C. Develop a heart of freedom in spontaneous worship unto God
3. Technical Skills - Offer your gift to the Lord and seek to be the best you can before God
   - A. Obedience and discipline are required
   - B. God called those who were skilled
   - C. Practice that which you have been given
   - D. Know your strengths, work on your weaknesses. Do not seek to dance beyond your capabilities

Spiritual Requirements include:
- The call of God
- A heart and vision for worship
- Character and Integrity
- Be established in the local church (Do you only show up when it is time to dance?)
- Be firmly established in the things of God, i.e. prayer, Word, Bible study
- Be submissive to church leadership and willing to take correction
- Be consistent, committed, diligent, faithful to attend

- rehearsals and practices
- Be willing to present your body a living sacrifice in general
- health (eating/exercise)
- Have a good attitude, be dependable and humble
- Study always to show yourself approved unto God

Do you want the anointing of God on your life? Of course you do. Let's look at a story about a woman named Mary with an alabaster box. In Mark 14:3-8, we are told that she worshipped Jesus by pouring the precious contents of an alabaster box on his feet. What did Jesus say? He said, "She has anointed me for my burial." True worship brought forth the anointing. When God anoints us, it is for our burial. The purpose of the anointing is for us to die to ourselves, so that we may minister dances of resurrection life. But the anointing is not just for Sunday service when we are in our dance garments. **The anointing is for our whole life.**

The same anointing that rest upon on Sunday morning should be with us when we are in school, at work or in the grocery store. The anointing is not something that can be faked. We must first be transparent with God, otherwise, we leave ourselves open to having areas not exposed to the light of God. The enemy hides in the darkness. God is calling us to a higher level of consecration in our daily lives and to a higher level of purpose in our dance. Only His presence and His anointing validate our expressions of worship. As we read God's Word, we see that the anointing was only placed on things that were consecrated - set apart for the service of God alone. High value was placed on an anointed object. The anointing will cost you everything. Therefore, we must let God deal with our foundations of our lives. There are no short cuts. Matthew 16:24 says, "If anyone desires to come after me, let him deny himself, and take up his cross, and follow me."

So we must worship from true hearts, for **worship is love responding to love.** We love Him because He first loved us. Worship will reveal our weaknesses and as we draw closer to God in worship, He can break us and we can begin to learn truer expressions of worship. Our hearts must be stirred to take hold of God - to follow hard after Him daily. The ultimate in worship is not the expression of our worship, but the knowledge of His presence. We will not experience the fullness of God when we reduce our expressions of worship to mere fleshly activities. Let's lay down our lives, seek God's heart and let dance be an anointed vehicle for the presence of God.

Once the ministry has begun, we can turn our attention to effective choreography. We must remember that we are not "just dancers" We are ministers of the Gospel and dance is God's Word in motion. Dance is a language and must be communicated clearly. Just as our fingerprints are different, our dance languages can be different. We must know how God desires to express Himself through us. We do not have to dance like anyone else. We have been created as special individuals in God's eyes. How does God dance through you? What are your strengths? Know your weaknesses and work to strengthen them. If you have never taken a ballet class, please do not try to incorporate ballet in your choreography. Don't try to dance beyond your capabilities.

While it does not say let them praise His name with dancing if you have taken lots of dance classes, we do know that God calls those who are skilled. Those who cannot play musical instruments are not placed over the music ministry as head musician to teach others what they do not know. Those who have no knowledge of singing are not called to lead a choir. Those who have no dance skill can only lead to a certain level. They can be great spiritual leaders, but it will take someone with knowledge of dance to help in other areas. If you believe God has called you to lead a dance ministry, perhaps you need to consider taking dance classes to keep yourself disciplined and prepared to lead others. If you decide to take dance classes, be careful what kind of classes you take. **I suggest taking a ballet class only because the technique required for ballet will help to strengthen your vessel and will help you to better express your dance language.**

Preparation must be spiritual as well as physical. If we seek God first, then He will direct us. He is the ultimate choreographer. We must become spiritually sensitive so as to avoid just filling time and space with movements that have no meaning.

Study the aesthetics of choreography. Be a student of the values of movements. Direct movements are movements that go to a direct place, a direct destination. Indirect movements are those that flow, those that have a more fluid quality. When do you use direct vs. indirect movements?

There are levels in choreography.
1. HUMILITY - Lying prostrate on the floor is the lowest level.
2. SUBMISSION - Kneeling with thighs resting on the feet (in a sitting position) is the next level.
3. YIELDED - Resting on the knees is the next level.
4. RESTORATION - Standing is the next level. From this level, you can lunge, which would be a bit lower, but still on the same level.
5. SEEKING - Releve means to rise (standing on the balls of the feet). This is the next level.
6. REJOICING - The next level actually involves leaving the floor, to jump or leap off of the floor.
7. ADVANCING involves remaining off the floor, perhaps using a prop to keep you elevated.

Always pray first to understand the various dynamics in choreography. Just as we do not talk all on one level of voice tone, so we must express the language of dance with levels, directions and dynamics -- strong movements vs. soft ones or heavy vs. light. Sometimes simple is better. Remember, it is not about the movements, it is about how to communicate God's message most effectively with the anointing of the Holy Spirit.

There are some questions we must ask ourselves:
- ✓ Is the dance truthful?
- ✓ Am I being honest in what I am expressing?
- ✓ What are the motivations for my movements?
- ✓ Am I communicating clearly?
- ✓ Are others being drawn into praise and worship?
- ✓ Does this glorify God and edify the body of Christ?
- ✓ Am I communicating the Spirit of the Gospel?

✓ Am I ministering decently and in order for the occasion?
✓ Am I willing to completely submit my heart and body to Jesus
   Christ for His purposes at all time?

When selecting music to dance to seek the Lord. Don't just dance to your favorite songs. Ask yourself these questions:

✓ Does it inspire others to praise and worship the Lord?
✓ Does it support the Word of God?
✓ Does it have too many words?
✓ Are the words easily understood?

Always get a clear copy of the song you are planning to use for ministry. If you use a CD, make sure there are no scratches on the CD. **It is important that the entire message, word movement and sound, is clearly communicated to God's people.** Determine to be excellent for the Lord.

Practical application:

1. Pray and ask the Lord to show you what Psalm to choreograph. Then ask Him to show you how to bring His Word to life.

2. Pray and ask the Lord what is the message on His heart to His people. Then ask Him to show you how He would have you to choreograph His message.

3. Pray and ask the Lord to give you an instrumental song to choreograph. Ask Him how to become the visual demonstration of what He wants to say through the sound of the music. Pray about incorporating worship instruments (billows, flags, etc.) that will best portray the message, but do not use them as a crutch if you do not know what movements to do.

4. Determine to develop a movement vocabulary. Below is a list of some choreographic elements. When preparing a message through movement, it is best to try to include as much as possible

in each ministry piece. Each element may not be appropriate for some messages, but with prayer and the creativity of the Holy Spirit, communicating a clear message can be achieved.

- Bowing
- Kneeling
- Walking (slow or fast)
- Running
- Turning
- Circling
- Leaping
- Jumping and hopping
- Skipping
- Changing directions
- Using different levels
- Dynamics (strong vs. soft, quick vs. sustained)
- Changing formations
- Covering Space

Also, your facial expressions are very important. What is experienced in the spirit should be communicated on your face! When we behold His glory, we cannot help but shine as a reflection of Him.

Practical Application:
Begin your time with God by obeying His call to worship. Prostrate yourself. That is always the best place to begin. Open your heart and allow Him to search it - for He desires truth in the inward parts. As you review this chapter, allow Him to speak to your heart. Be willing to make any corrections or changes that He might reveal to you. Then rise up and walk in obedience. Isaiah 1:19 tells us that if we are "willing and obedient" we will "eat the good of the land."

NOTE: The Choreography DVD, *Bringing Your Dance to Life* by Apostle Pamela would be a good tool to add to your library. It will assist you in developing your movement vocabulary.

Chapter Ten

HOLY GARMENTS AND THE PRIESTHOOD

As New Testament priests, we are called to minister in the tabernacle of the Lord. Take some time and study Exodus Chapter 28. You will see that God was very specific about the garments that He wanted the priests to wear. As we serve God in this ministry, let us realize that we do not wear "costumes" or "outfits, "we wear priestly garments - Holy garments. We must begin to see the importance of the garments we wear.

Let's look at who was consecrated and set apart to wear these garments. Exodus 28:1-6 reads as such:

> *"Now take Aaron your brother, and his sons with him, from among the children of Israel, that he may minister to me as priests, Aaron and Aaron's sons: Nadab, Abihu, Eleazar, and Ithamar. And you shall make holy garments for Aaron our brother, for glory and for beauty. So you shall speak to all who are gifted artisans, whom I have filled with the spirit of wisdom, that they may make Aaron's garments, to consecrate him, that he may minister to Me as priest. And these are the garments which they shall make: a breastplate, an ephod, a robe, a skillfully woven tunic, a turban, and a sash. So they shall make holy garments for Aaron your brother and his sons, that they may minister to me as priest. They shall take the gold, blue, purple, and scarlet thread, and the fine linen, and they shall make the*

ephod of gold, blue, purple, and scarlet thread and fine woven linen, artistically worked."

You will notice in verse 1, Aaron and his sons were to be set apart in order to minister unto the Lord. As stated earlier, ministry to the Lord is always our first priority. **We are called to minister unto Him first, and then we will be prepared to answer the call to minister for Him in the dance.**

The Aaronic priesthood qualified Aaron and his sons to minister unto the Lord. The claim for this office of the priesthood was sonship. Their work was to minister in the holy things of God each day in the Tabernacle. That was their first priority. I believe that everyone is called to dance before the Lord, but not everyone is called to minister in dance before God's people. We must be called. Also, we must live a consecrated life, wholly set apart for God. If we have no private ministry unto the Lord, we should not have a public one!

The time of ministry unto the Lord in the hidden, secret place is crucial. Proverbs 8:34-35 says, "Blessed is the man who listens to me, watching daily at my gates, waiting at the posts of my doors. For he shall find life and obtain favor from the Lord." I challenge you now - if you do not have a consistent daily time in the presence of the Lord, now is the time to begin. I continue to make mention of this because it is the most important. Make that your priority. Get up earlier, stay up later, allow no distractions. Be consistent in meeting with God daily. It will change your life. Psalm 91 says, He who **dwells** in the secret place...," not he who visits the secret place. Abiding in Christ must be our daily worship. We must not wait until Sunday morning to meet with Him. He is our daily habitation and we are His temple.

The words *"that they may minister unto me"* are repeated two more times in the next five verses. I believe this is repeated so we will be careful not to lose our focus as to why we are called. Verse two says, they shall have HOLY garments. Our garments are Holy. To be Holy means to be set apart. They only wore these garments when they went into the temple to worship. They were not to be worn for everyday use. That means we must treat them as Holy. We do not treat them as just another piece of clothing. We purposefully take care of them, clean them and make sure they are prepared for the next time we need them. Verse two also says that the garments are for GLORY and for BEAUTY. **Pray and seek God about what He would have you to wear.** Let us not allow our garment to be a disservice to our ministry or to the message God desires to speak through us. Our garments are to be for God's glory that they may reflect the beauty of the Lord. Vivien Hibbert says, "We are carriers of the sights of God." This includes our garments.

Verse three tells us that those who were wise hearted were called upon to make the garments. In other words, God was very specific about what He wanted the Priests to wear as they ministered unto Him in the temple. He did not say, "just go and get whatever you want and put it on. If you like it, I will like it." It was and still is important to Him. We must pray and be willing to walk in obedience to Gods purposes no matter what the cost. We must desire garments that will reflect the glory and the beauty of our Lord. We must serve Him with a spirit of excellence. He is worth it. It may mean that we have to make some sacrifice in order to have proper garments that will reflect His beauty and His glory. Verse three goes on to say that our garments are a part of our consecration to the ministry. To be consecrated means to be set apart. Our garments are part of what sets us apart for ministry unto the Lord.

Study the consecration of Aaron and his sons in Exodus 29. It tells us in verse 20 that the blood was applied to the right ear, the right thumb on the right hand and the great toe of the right foot. The blood was applied to the ear because God wanted them to hear His voice, not other voices. Today, we must be careful to protect our ear gates. We have many voices competing with the voice of the Lord, so I ears must be tuned to His voice.

God will hear the confessions and petitions of His people if we will hear Him and hearken to His voice alone. The blood was applied to the thumb on the right hand, so that the people could do the work of God and handle the things of God with Holy hands. God does not want our dirty hands on His Holy things! Let us never seek to serve the Lord for personal gain.

The blood was applied to the great toe on the right foot so the people would walk in His ways and minister unto Him for His glory.

Verse 21 tells us that the blood and the anointing oil were sprinkled on Aaron and on his garments, on his sons and on their garments. It then says that he and his garments are holy, and his sons and their garments are also holy.

Exodus 28, verse 4 says, "...and these are the garments..." I suggest you do an extensive study on each piece of the priestly garments. Each piece speaks to us of an aspect of Jesus Christ. And when the priests were adorning themselves with the garments, they put them on in a specific order.

First, was the coat with the girdle. It was made of fine linen of purest white. The girdle was a symbol of service. It speaks to us abut the truth that we must always have a proper attitude of being ready for action. Next, was the robe of the ephod. It was to be blue. A robe symbolized the office and the authority to fulfill the requirements of the office. It was associated with dignity and royalty. The robes had ornaments of golden bells and pomegranates on the hem that were symbols of the gifts of the Spirit and the fruit of the Spirit respectively. The pomegranates were placed in between the bells to keep them from clashing against each other.

Afterward were the ephod and the curious girdle. They connected the breastplate. Inside of the breastplate were the Urim and the Thummin. These were stones given to the priests to seek the mind of God and to reveal the will of God. The girdle was used to strengthen the loins. It speaks of our need to be equipped. Next was the breastplate of judgment which was worn on the outside to cover the heart. Twelve precious stones were arranged in order according to the 12 tribes. Following that was the mitre and the bonnets. They crowned the head as symbols of holiness and righteousness. They represented the authority of the Priests. The bonnet signified submission and covered the head while in the presence God. With the mitre was a plate of pure gold. It read

HOLINESS UNTO THE LORD. It was placed on the forehead, the seat of the will, mind and intellect. 1 Peter 1:15 admonishes us to "be holy in all your conduct." The breeches were made of linen. This represents that we must dress modestly and in decency. God told them to cover their nakedness and their flesh.

When ministering to the Lord in the congregation, we are representing Him. Therefore, we must be very careful not to wear garments that are too tight fitting or garments that are revealing. Garments that cling to the body, or see through or low cut will not represent the Holiness of our God. We are to be covered in His Holiness, not only in dress, but in our service, in our thoughts, and in all areas of life.

Much detail was given to the making of the garments. Each piece spoke of the truth and the character of Jesus Christ. Quality mattered! God instructed them to use fine linen. The coat with the girdle was to be made of fine linen and was to be pure white. The fabric was of such fine quality. It is not available to us today. This is considered the foundational garment. It speaks of righteousness and holiness. Is 61:10 says, "...For He has clothed me with the garments of salvation, He has covered me with the robe of righteousness..."

The girdle, the bonnet, and the breaches are also symbols of our service unto the Lord. We must be ready in our attitude and in our actions, and their loins must be girded. Isaiah 11:5 states, "Righteousness shall be the belt of His loins, and faithfulness the belt of His waist."

The robe of the Ephod was to be a specific color - blue. The robe symbolized the office and the authority of the office of the priesthood. It was associated with dignity and royalty. The blue robe represented grace. It covered the white foundational garment which represented righteousness and the law.

In verse five, God is specific about the colors that He wants to be a part of the priestly garments: Gold, Blue, Purple and Scarlet. Again, each color represents an aspect of God. Gold represents the deity of Christ, the fact that He is God all by Himself. He is God and there is no other. He is the

Omnipotent, Omniscient, Omnipresent, all-powerful, all-knowing, ever present God. Blue represents heavenly things and the Holy Spirit as well as grace and divinity. Purple represents royalty. It also represents the combination of His divinity and His humanity. Scarlet represents His passion. It represents the fact that Jesus poured out His very life for us.

Spend time with God. Find out how He wants to display His glory and His beauty through your garments. Cry out to God for a manifestation of His presence that is real. We cannot duplicate the anointing. We cannot fake it. Even the best of garments cannot cover up for a life that is not holy.

God never called those to the priesthood who were not consecrated unto Him. Leviticus 21 outlines the regulations for the conduct and call of the priests. Verses 18-20 tell us that anyone who had a defect could not approach to make offerings unto the Lord. Anyone who was blind (unable to see spiritual things) or lame (unable to walk in the ways of the Lord), who had a flat nose (having no discernment) or anything superfluous (reflects a lack of balance).

It goes on to say, "a man that is broken footed (unstable in the ways of the Lord), or broken handed (one who walks in selfishness who will not reach out his hand to help another), or is crookback (unable to walk upright), or a dwarf (one who refuses to grow up in the things of God), or a man who has a blemish in his eye (we judge others when we have a plank in our own eye), or scurvy (one who has itching ears), or scabbed (one who refused to allow offenses or wounds to heal properly) or has his stones broken (one who is unable to reproduce the life of God).

Once we understand that we are called, consecrated and clothed for the Glory of God, He will commission us as priests and send us forth to do the work of the Kingdom. Romans 13:14 tells us to "put on the Lord Jesus Christ and make no provision for the flesh." When we live in the anointing of the Lord, not only can we put on "the garment of praise for the spirit of heaviness," but we can help others to put on this same garment of praise.

These are the Garments, a book by Charles W. Slemming is a great resource for study on garments.

Chapter Eleven

Skill Versus Anointing - The Role of Skill in Worship

Skill in any art form is beautiful. We pay $100 per ticket to go to the theatre to hear the best singer, see the best actors, and watch the best dancers. What we hear - what we see is beautiful. What we do not do; however, pay to see those who are not skillful in their craft. The world recognizes discipline and skill. There is an appreciation given to those who have taken time to study and attain a certain level of skill and artistry, and they are rewarded for their gifts and talents. While we do not measure ourselves as the world does, shouldn't we desire to bring offerings of skill and beauty to the ONE who created all things? We should not expect that because dance is in the church, it is less than excellent.

God is a God of order and His creation is filled with beauty. God did not just throw things together. The ocean knows where to stop. The next time you are near the ocean, pause and listen to the song of the waves and watch them dance as they beat against the rocks. Or listen to the song of the wind in the trees and watch their dance of praise as they blow in the wind.

When you look at the arts as we know them today, they are divided into different forms, i.e., dance, music, drama, etc. However, they were not divided into separate entities until the end of the 1st millennium A.D. Singing, music and dance were all one. When you look at pictures from ancient Egyptian art shows, you will see groups often in a procession, not sitting in chairs or in a choir loft as we see them today. There were no specialties then, so references to vocal, instrumental or dance was a reference to all three. Most ancient writers say that dance did not play a big role, but when you put it all together; some type of movement was often implied when there were psalms, hymns and spiritual songs.

Evidence from ancient archeology depicts a culture that included all the art forms, often being expressed at the same time. Hieroglyphics show men with harps in procession, hands holding clashing symbols or playing a stringed instrument, feet in the air as if in stride or dancing and mouths open as if singing - all at the same time. A standard picture often seen is of girls playing double pipes (known as a recorder) with a single mouth piece, doing some kind of movement or dance. Exodus 15:20 is the first mention of dance in the scriptures. Miriam sang while she danced and played a tambourine. **Shall we conclude that the prophetic anointing blends the divine enablement with human expressions through the arts?**

There is no place in the Word of God that tells us to sit and watch people dance. When you look at musical depictions in scriptures, community movements were implied. Dance was always a form of worship for the entire community because dance and music is indigenous to every culture. In ancient times, they did not sit in a theater format as we do today. Today, our culture breeds performance. There is a performance mentality that has crept into the church. Many see talent and call it the anointing. Man cannot duplicate that which only comes from the Spirit of God. We must cry out for that which is real and authentic. **Let God anoint what you have trained.**

We are all called to sing and make a joyful noise unto the Lord, but we are not all called to sing before God's people. The Bible encourages us to dance before the Lord, but not all are called to dance before the Lord's people. It takes skill to play any instrument. So why have God's people chosen to settle for mediocrity and artistic slothfulness instead of taking the time to study and prepare to bring an offering of beauty to the Lord?

The Bible tells us in Psalm 33 that praise is comely for the upright. The scriptures go on to say "Play skillfully with a loud noise." Does this not imply training? 1 Chronicles chapter 15 says that those who were skilled were separated for service. In other words, you may have a natural gift but you still need training. **Developing the gifts God has given to you is part of being a good steward.** The parable of the talents explains that very well. Training helps us to maximize what God gave us. Be a good steward of the seed of talent God has entrusted to you.

There is a debate in the church today among many dance ministers -- Should I take class or not? Do I have to take class to dance for the Lord? I believe that we all should do all we can to be the best that we can be for the Lord. Taking classes is a means to an end, the end being to bring glory to the Lord, not to ourselves. We must not allow skill to become an idol. Then it becomes the end instead of just the means to an end. **Talent without anointing is just pretty to look at.** Anointing without skill is still lacking in the full power of its potential. But instruction brings order and discipline defines the gift. When you combine skill with the anointing, you have a full meal for others to partake of and they will be well fed. That is how we, too, can become the bread of life for others.

The truth is I cannot glorify God through music on a violin or a trumpet because my particular skill is as a dancer. The variable here is the skill. The more developed the skill, the more liberty there is. Limitations are less. Discipline and training bring a liberty that cannot be expressed in the same way as one who has less training. However, more training does not necessarily bring more of an anointing. I cannot tell you how to read sheet music for an entire orchestra, so chances are, I would not be a candidate to lead the music ministry. I cannot tell you how tenors and altos and sopranos are to work together in perfect harmony. Therefore, I would not be a good candidate to be a choir director. So why is it that we allow anyone to lead our dance ministries when it is often clear that dance is not their primary gift? Once we know the purpose of dance and how that relates to God's call on our lives, we will not continue to try to lead in areas where we are not equipped.

I believe that dance is a language that we must learn to speak clearly so we can become clear, prophetic demonstrations of what God is saying and doing. Just as the trumpet must make a clear sound so the people will know to gather for war or for worship, so our dances must have clarity in our expression. Music is not loud all the time. In an orchestra, each instrument does not play always at the same time. Without the clear sound, it would be chaos. For example, just as one singer has a different dynamic than a choir, so one instrument has a different dynamic than an orchestra. So we must study dynamics, levels, directions (see chapter on choreography) in order to bring the clarity necessary for dance.

Skill and training also bring control. When music is out of tune, singers are off pitch or dancers have no body alignment, we show that we are not skilled in our craft - not disciplined in our expressions of worship to the Lord. Did David stop to take a dance class? Did Miriam stop to learn the five positions of ballet? No but they were dancing before God, not before His people as His representative to a lost and dying world. **Dance is ministry.**

There is prayer closet worship that is only meant to bless the heart of God and no one else. Then, there is dance as ministry to others. Should it be the same thing? Do evangelists preach to themselves all the time in their prayer time? No. They shut in with God to worship Him, draw near, then go and share His messages with others. Does your pastor come from His prayer closet only to speak to God and ignore the congregation every Sunday morning? No! Dance as ministry works in much the same way. We spend time with Him, study to show ourselves approved unto Him, then we go out and change the world through our dance. People do not want to watch us worship. They want to join us in worship. Also, we are not there to perform or pretend that we are in our private time when we are before people. We are there to preach His messages through movement. Let's study so we can be clear in the messages we are preaching.

Skill also produces patience and self control. You cannot learn all there is to know over night. You can settle for playing chopsticks or you can develop skill that will allow you to become a world class concerto. You can dance in the corp de ballet or you can develop skill that will allow you to be a primary dancer - a soloist.

Discipline reflects our attitude toward God and the worship experience. In 1 Chronicles 21, we read the story of King David. He numbered the people and God became angry with him. He sent a plague among the people. David then went to buy the threshing floor to build an altar and bring a sacrifice to God. Araunah the Jebusite offered to give David the threshing floor. David's reply was, "I will not offer burnt offerings unto the Lord my God which cost me nothing." Discipline in any area shows God how much we value Him, His house, His people and the worship experience as a whole.

Psalm 78:72 says, "And David shepherded them with integrity of heart; with skillful hands he led them." Leaders are often distinguished by their discipline and skill, especially when accompanied by a Godly lifestyle.

Skill also allows you to be confident in what you are expressing. It will quiet the voice of insecurity. However, humble people are realistic. They realize that there are always people who are better than they are. They learn from others and are not afraid to receive constructive feedback. **Arrogance mixed with skill can be the very thing that turns others away from Christ instead of bringing them into the presence of God through anointed worship.** Learn to be sensitive to the presence of the Lord in the midst of His people.

Determine to be your best for the ONE who gave us all His best. Determine to serve Him with humility and excellence. Ask the Lord what skills He wants you to focus on. Then be obedient and commit to follow through because of your love for the Lord. May we all have a fiery passion to make His praises glorious!

Chapter Twelve

FLOWING IN PROPHETIC DANCE

We live in a day of increased revelation. Revelation 19:10 says, "...worship God. For the testimony of Jesus is the spirit of prophecy." Prophecy is the voice of God - of revelation and illumination, revealing the mind of Christ. In these end-times, God is moving by His Spirit like never before. Will we move with Him or remain in our man-made traditions? Acts 2:17 says, "And it shall come to pass in the last days, says God, That I will pour out of My Spirit on all flesh; Your sons and your daughters SHALL prophesy..."

God is calling people who will be like the sons of Issachar in 1 Chronicles 12:32. The sons of Issachar were men that had understanding of times, and they knew what Israel was to do. In this hour, God is calling forth a prophetic people who will hear from heaven and then speak and demonstrate the purposes of God.

There is the office of the Prophet and there is the gift of Prophecy. According to Revelation 19:10, there is the spirit of prophecy. You may not be called to the office of the prophet or you may not have the gift of prophecy, but the Holy Spirit who lives inside of you is a prophetic Spirit. That makes you a prophetic instrument in the hand of the Lord. When the Spirit of God is moving mightily in the midst of His people, He may call you forth to dance, to speak or to sing a word of prophecy from the Lord.

Because the testimony of Jesus is the Spirit of Prophecy, any Spirit-filled believer who is sensitive to the presence of God may operate in the Spirit of prophecy.

The prophetic is the very life and breath of God in our midst. Have you ever heard the Lord speak to you and say, "Go dance," as you worshipped Him in a Sunday service? At the time you heard the voice, you were not sure if it was the Lord or not, so you stood there and asked, "Is that you Lord? Is that you?" You ask yourself, "Should I go dance?" Then you say to yourself, "Give me a sign, Lord! Let me know that it is really you." Just at that moment, someone else may respond to the Lord and then you realize it really was the Lord speaking to you. We must realize that God wants to communicate with His people and He wants to speak through us to bring forth His messages and minister to His people.

If you have the liberty to minister in dance during praise and worship in a spontaneous manner, you must still learn to be discerning. **Just because the music is playing does not always mean you need to dance.** We want to avoid becoming a distraction by dancing to every song, all the time. Learn to discern the voice of the Lord and to know when He may want or not want dance to go forth. In other words, if you have the liberty to move out in dance, be obedient to the Holy Spirit, but do not dance just because there is music or singing.

Everyone on the dance team does not need to dance all together all the time. There may be times when God will call for one dancer or perhaps only two or three. Sometimes He will lead you to move separately, and sometimes simultaneously. Think of an orchestra. There are times when all the instruments play together harmoniously, and there are other times when the flute, the drums or the piano may have a solo, depending on what sound needs to come forth, what message needs to be communicated.

Submission to leadership is also a must. There may be times when you may be called on to go forth and minister. At those times you must trust your leadership and trust God that you will indeed be led by the Spirit of God to dance His message. **The Dance Minister has the ability to shift**

the atmosphere. You do not need to be in the office of the Prophet to flow in the Prophetic.

To prophesy means:
- To speak by divine inspiration
- To fore-tell that which is to come (about a future event)
- To forth-tell (telling a truth)
- To agree with what God has already said to be true in His Word

So prophesy sometimes means to forth-tell that which is coming, i.e., "Thus saith the Lord..." It may mean to make a spiritual prediction or to speak under divine inspiration. Other times, to prophesy can mean to preach infallibly or to speak forth that which God has already said to be true. For example, if you are dancing to a song based on Revelation 11:15, "The Kingdoms of the world are become the Kingdoms of our Lord and of His Christ; and He will reign forever and ever..." We know those words are true. Even though we have not seen it come to pass yet, we know it shall be true. Therefore, because God says it shall be so, our dance falls under the umbrella of the spirit of Prophecy. It is a Prophetic Dance. **Therefore, prophetic dance can be spontaneous or choreographed.**

Prophetic dance can also come forth before, during or after the Word of the Lord and can precede the Word. If it stands alone, with or without instrumental music or without word interpretation, it must communicate a very clear message from God. Prophetic dance may or may not be accompanied by a word or a song and may or may not incorporate tools, such as flags or streamers. However, the use of such worship tools can be used to greatly increase the effectiveness of the message you desire to bring forth. The physical becomes an extension of the spiritual thereby becoming a prophetic demonstration.

I Corinthians 14:1-5 states, "Pursue love, and desire spiritual *gifts*, but especially that you may prophesy. For he who speaks in a tongue does not speak to men but to God, for no one understands *him;* however, in the spirit he speaks mysteries. But he who prophesies speaks edification and exhortation and comfort to men. He who speaks in a tongue edifies himself, but he who prophesies edifies the church. I wish you all spoke with tongues, but even more that you prophesied; for he who prophesies *is* greater than he who speaks with tongues, unless indeed he interprets, that the church may receive edification."

Verse one tells us that we should desire to prophesy. Verse three tells us the three-fold purpose of prophecy - edification, exhortation and comfort unto men. Tongues is unto God, prophecy is unto men. To edify means to **build up.** To exhort means to **encourage.** God comforts us so we may comfort others. Any prophecy, whether word, song or dance must edify, exhort and/or comfort. That is how you discern if it is truly a prophetic word from God. Ask yourself - does it edify? Does it exhort? Does it comfort? **The Holy Spirit inside of you is a prophetic Spirit and He will minister through you.** Romans 12:6 encourages us to prophesy according to the proportion of our faith.

Discerning the voice of the Lord is of the utmost importance, but you must trust God to lead you. In John 10:4-5, Jesus says His sheep hear His voice and know His voice and the voice of a stranger they will not follow. He wants us to know that which is pure real and true so we can avoid deception that comes from false prophets. In 1 Thessalonians 5:20, it shares with us that we should not despise prophecy. Rather, we are to desire to prophesy. Allow the Lord to minister and to dance His dances through you.

To prepare yourself for prophetic expression, you must:
>   A. Know the Word of God to obey the Word of God
>   - Jeremiah 31:13 -- ...the virgin (bride) shall rejoice in the dance
>   - Exodus 15:20 - Miriam led the dance because of her relationship to the deliverer
>   - Psalm 149:3 – Psalm 150:4 (machowl – congregational dances done in circles)
>   - Zephaniah 3:17 -- The Lord rejoices over us (spins around under the influence of a violent emotion)
>   - I Chronicles 15 - We have been appointed as carriers of the ark (presence) of God

B. Check the motives of your heart

      The dance of Salome was manipulative. She danced to get what she wanted from the King. The end result was the head of John the Baptist on a platter

C. Learn to listen - John 10:27

D. Know when to dance - wait on The Lord to lead and to guide

      Vivien Hibbert says, "Dancers are carriers of the sights of God. Musicians are carriers of the sounds of God, and Psalmists are carriers of the words of God."

Having revelation to know when to move out in dance can come as:

- Obeying an impression or feeling
- Listening for the still small voice
- Hearing an internal audible voice
- Hearing an external audible voice
- Responding to a sermon or teaching (prepared vs. spontaneous dances)
- Having a vision
- Seeing a picture - i.e., a response to instrumental music (movement must communicate clearly)
- Being obedient to leadership

E. Prophetic Ministry takes place in three realms – Colossians 2:15

- Heavens unto God – Psalms 23:1
- Unto principalities and powers - Ephesians 3:10
- Earth realm – Jeremiah 29:11; Isaiah 61:1-11
- David encouraged himself in the Lord – I Samuel 30:6
- Edify, exhort and encourage yourself and others

F. Using Instruments to accompany prophetic movement (visual demonstrations)

Examples: A sword
A shield
A cloth
A Bible
A matte
A tambourine
A candle
Flags
Banners
A Rain stick
Billows
A crown
A scepter

G. Understanding Colors and What They Represent – examples are:

Gold – The Deity of Christ

Silver – Redemption/Bronze – Refinement

Black – Death, Famine, Peril – other times, warfare

Green – Everlasting Life, Prosperity

Purple - Royalty

Scarlet – The Passion of Christ, His Humanity

Blue – Heavenly Things, Refreshing River, Holy Spirit

Red – The blood of Jesus

Rainbow – Covenant

White – Holiness, Purity, Light, Righteousness

Prophetic movements are the movements of God. They are the movements that come from His heart, from His throne - movements that begin in the Spirit realm that God releases to us here on earth to accomplish His purposes. God is calling a people who will know the times and the seasons and know what to do. Revelation 19:10 says the testimony of Jesus is the spirit of prophecy.

He is calling a prophetic people, who will hear Him, speak His words and demonstrate His purposes.

Prophetic ministry is the heart of God revealed to us or revealed through us. We are called to be prophetic enactments of the Holy Spirit; called to be visual demonstrations of what God is saying and doing. God has dances from heaven that He wants to dance through us to bring change and meet the needs of people.

These dances are Spirit to Spirit. **When we allow God's movements to flow through us, we will see signs follow.** We will see people healed, delivered and set free by His power. We will see people brought into a new dimension in Christ. As the physical becomes an extension of the spiritual, God's power is released in the earth upon the hearts of men. Healing, deliverance, prosperity, peace, joy and all that we need to live abundant lives has already been established in heaven, we just have to know how to access them. I believe we can reach up into the heavens and by faith pull down those things that God has provided for us.

Amos 9:11 and Acts 15:16 tell us that the restoration of the Tabernacle of David is so that we might possess the remnant. The word *possess* is the Hebrew word yaresh. It literally means to occupy by driving out the previous tenants. In other words, we can declare God's healing where there is sickness. We can declare God's deliverance where there is bondage. We do this by the spoken Word of God. Jesus said, "My words are spirit and they are life."

God's Word never returns void of that which He purposes. Deliverance will come as we lift our voices in praise to God. As we use our hands to smite the enemy. Clapping our hands is associated with praise, but also with smiting the enemy. God told the prophet Ezekiel to smite with his hands and stamp with his feet. This was a sign of God's judgment against Israel for the sins they had committed in His sight. Our feet represent authority. He has given us every piece of ground the soles of our feet will tread upon. Luke, Chapter 10 says, we trample on serpents and scorpions and on all the power of the enemy and nothing shall harm us. According to Psalm 18, God has given us the necks of our enemies. These are prophetic movements of the body as we yield to Him.

Dance in the church today is a fulfillment of prophecy. Jeremiah 31:13 says that in the last days the virgin shall rejoice in the dance. The word *virgin* in this scripture is the word bride. We are preparing ourselves to be His bride. Revelation 19:7 says, let us rejoice and be glad, for the marriage supper of the lamb has come and the bride has made herself ready. In these last days, we will see God rebuilding His church, preparing His bride.

In the book of Exodus, God miraculously delivered the children of Israel from many years in bondage to Pharaoh. He brought them through the Red Sea. This represents the fact that we have been delivered from sin, death, hell, sickness and the grave itself. We have been brought through the blood of Jesus. Miriam, the Prophetess, led the women in the dance. It was a custom in those days for the closest female relative to meet and to greet a returning victor after a battle. Miriam was the closest female relative to Moses. And as His bride, we are the closest female relative to Jesus. He is our returning victor. He has won the victory and we demonstrate His authority in the earth.

The Feast of Tabernacles, the Feast of His coming, was a main event associated with dance in Israel. As His return gets closer, we will dance more and more. We will say to God, we are your bride. We know you are the victor, and we are making ourselves ready. Our dancing says to the world, He is coming – get ready. Our dancing says to the enemy, your time is short. Our dancing says to each other, see the vision, have faith.

As we testify to one another of the goodness and provision of God, we yield to the Spirit of prophecy, for the testimony of Jesus is the Spirit of Prophecy.

Chapter Thirteen

REAL MEN DANCE!

King David was a worshipper. In 2 Samuel 6 and again in I Chronicles 13 and 15, we read about this dancing King named David. You may know the story. While Saul was King, the ark of God, which represented the presence of God in the midst of His people, was not in Israel. Saul had not sought after the ark during his reign as King. When David became King, he knew that the ark of God needed to be restored to His people. So, David sought after the ark which had been in the house of Obed-Edom. The house of Obed-Edom was richly blessed while the ark was there and David set his heart to bring the ark back to its proper place.

As they were bringing the ark back to its proper place, they placed the ark on a new cart. All of Israel played music before the Lord. What was to be a celebration turned into a tragedy. The oxen carrying the cart stumbled. As Uzzah put forth his hand to steady the ark, the anger of the Lord arose and he struck Uzzah. Uzzah died on the spot. Can you imagine the terror that must have come to all who were gathered there? The Bible says David became angry and was afraid of God. Then he asked this question: "How can the ark of the Lord come to me?" The ark was then taken to the house of Obed-Edom, the Gittite. It stayed there for three months and God blessed the house of Obed-Edom because of the ark. So David went and brought up the ark with gladness. We must all ask ourselves the same question: "How can the ark of the Lord come to me?" Many people, many churches are seeking to carry the ark without realizing that the ark is not present in their midst. Tradition, religion and other man-made ideas have kept the ark from being with them. We sense that the "oxen has stumbled" when we think things have gotten out of order according to our standards or beliefs so we reach out our hands to steady the presence of God. The anger of God is aroused when we begin to touch what belongs to Him. He does not want us to touch what belongs to Him alone. So churches die, ministries die, as the presence of the Lord is no longer there. So David did what we all must do - protect the presence of the Lord.

As we read verse one of 1 Chronicles 15, we see that David prepared a place for the ark and pitched a tent for it. We are to be the prepared place for the presence of the Lord. It states in verse two that "No one can carry the ark of God, but the Levites, for the Lord has chosen them to carry the ark of God and to minister before Him forever. We are also a "chosen generation" called by God to carry His presence and to minister unto Him. **Those who do not know God cannot carry the presence of God.** Only those He has chosen can carry His presence, those who will daily prepare a place for the ark.

All of Israel, men, women and children alike, gathered to bring up the ark of the Lord, but David instructed the heads of the fathers' houses of the Levites to sanctify themselves so they could bring up the ark to the place that had been prepared for it. Verse 14 of the same chapter says that the priests and the Levites were sanctified. They set themselves apart unto God.

As they bore the ark of God on their shoulders as Moses had commanded them, King David appointed those who were skilled to play music on various instruments. Among them were cymbals, harps, strings and trumpets.

2 Samuel 6:13-14 says, "And so it was, when those bearing the ark of the Lord had gone six paces, that he sacrificed oxen and fatted sheep. Then David danced before the Lord with all his might:"

The Hebrew word for dance in 2 Samuel 6:4 is KARAR, meaning to whirl about! Just imagine the King of Israel, leaping and stamping, whirling about wildly for joy before the Lord. 1 Chronicles 15:29 uses the word *dancing*. The Hebrew word used there is is *raqad*, meaning to stamp, to spring about wildly for joy, to jump, leap and skip.

I believe that's what King David experienced in his spirit, then demonstrated with his body. God accepted their sacrifices and the presence of God was once again in its rightful place - in the midst of God's people.

As we prepare our hearts for the presence of the Lord and sanctify ourselves, we, too, men and women alike can usher in the ark of the Lord and be carriers of the very presence of God. The King of Israel led the entire nation in worship. **Pray for the spirit of David to be released in our churches, from the Pastor to the choir loft to the men sitting in the back pew.** The power of God is released when the men dance. Ask the Lord to send His freedom to the men in the body of Christ, so they can prepare a place for the ark of God and lead in worship as King David did.

The story tells us that Michal, the wife of David, saw him "whirling and playing music; and she despised him in her heart." I believe that Michal missed the presence of God and focused on the dance. We must endeavor to always have the presence of God as our top priority. We want others to see God in the midst of our dance. Our dance should never be the focal point. For King David, the ark was truly the center of attention. How unfortunate that when we minister before the Lord, there are those who will choose not to see God's presence in our midst. Nevertheless, we can respond as David did -- "It was before the Lord, who chose me...therefore I will play music before the Lord."

Men! Know that God has called you and chosen you to minister to Him. Don't let anyone despise your worship. You are free to dance like David danced!

During one of my visits to Israel, I was at the Western Wall at the end of the Holy day. The Rabbi came out to blow the Shofar to signify the end of

Yom Kippur? What I saw next truly amazed me! Many Jewish men came dancing down to the wall to celebrate the fact that their sins had been atoned for one more year.

On another visit to the Holy Land, we went to the Western Wall at the beginning of Shabat. I understand that it is a tradition for the families to gather to pray at the Wall every Friday just before sundown. Again, I saw many Jewish men doing exactly what Psalm 149:3 and Psalm 150:4 instruct us to do: Let them praise His name with dancing!

The word *dance* in that scripture means the **round dance.** As they came together to celebrate the goodness of the Lord, they danced together in circles. These dances took place around an altar or at a feast. They were part of their everyday life. The men danced, the women danced, the children danced, often in a circle together.

I was seeing the scripture come to life. I could hear the dancing before I could see it. Then once I arrived at the wall, the sight was incredible. Circles of Jewish men were dancing and singing with the ladies also in circles and their children among them! They sang as they danced and celebrated the Lord.

As I gazed in amazement at this sight, my heart yearned for the men in the body of Christ to rise up and lead us all in dances of victory because the Lamb of God has been slain from before the foundations of the earth and our sins are indeed atoned for, not for one more year, but once and for all. The ultimate sacrifice has been made on the cross. I pray for our men to be released into all the fullness of every expression of worship unto the Lord. We need our men to lead us. They reflect an aspect of God that women cannot display. Religious tradition has been responsible for telling men that they are not free to express their love for God through dance. As I travel, I see this more and more, but particularly in our western culture. I have seen many more men free to dance in Latin American countries, such as Costa Rica, Mexico and Puerto Rico. How awesome to see men dancing before God, even as David danced.

In the New Testament, we read about a man named Prochorus. Acts 6:1-5 says they chose men who were of good reputation, full of the Holy Spirit and wisdom to set over business affairs. The name Prochorus gives us an insight into an aspect of what his ministry was. Pro means leader and chorus means the round dance. More than likely, he was a leader of the round dance.

In Luke, Chapter 15, we are told of the parable of the lost son. After the son had left home, journeyed to a far country and wasted his possessions on an ungodly lifestyle, the Bible says he "came to himself" and decided to return to his father. His father was so filled with compassion that he decided to celebrate the return of his son. The oldest son was in the field and as he drew near to the house, and it is recorded that he "heard music and dancing." It does not state that he heard music and saw dancing! What was it that he heard? Was it the sound of hands clapping? Was it the sound of feet shuffling?

As I witnessed dancing at the Western Wall in Jerusalem, there seemed to be a shift in the atmosphere when dancing took place. An excitement filled the air that seemed to be tangible. I believe that is what the oldest son heard. For me it was the sound of a joyful heart anticipating an encounter with the King of Kings. Because dance was a part of their lives, especially at times of celebration, it would not have been out of place to see the men dancing. Ancient writings recorded that Jesus danced at the wedding at Cana. After all, dancing is a tradition at weddings. Why would the wedding at Cana be any different?

Ancient writings also record that Jesus danced with His disciples at the last supper. I believe that even though He knew what was ahead for Him, he chose to celebrate this time with His disciples. He chose to set joy before Him.

We serve a God of movement. It brings joy to His heart when we abandon ourselves in worship before His throne.

<u>Words From Christopher Hardy</u>

Men! Dance and Worship your way into **Unlimited Possibilities**

Men, there is a war for your **FREEDOM!** Dance and worship always allows you to express your freedom.

Imagine walking, talking and communing with the Spirit of God all day long. That is how it was with Adam and Eve in the Garden. Their communion was so powerful that work and worship became one! This perfect place of worship caused the garden to prosper. That was and still is the ultimate plan of God. That was a place of **Unlimited Possibilities.** Satan hated this perfect communion. He knows the power we have in the earth realm when we truly walk and talk with the Lord. Therefore, he had to find a way to interrupt the prosperity of the garden and he is still busy trying to interrupt out communion with God.

The true worshipper has no gender. The true worshipper has a kingdom mentality because we are in the King's domain and under His rule! Since worship is a kingdom experience, you and I must determine to have a desire to worship our king with complete freedom! I Peter 2:6 says, "We are a chosen generation, a royal priesthood, a holy nation, a special people..." this tells me that **we are chosen for true worship!**

To be a true worshipper we must understand who it is that we worship.
1. Worship is not an emotional experience - it's a lifestyle at all times. **Matt. 22:37 says, "Love the Lord with all your heart, soul and mind."**

2. Worship is an act of humility, submitting ourselves to God. **II Chronicles 7:14 says, Seek God and humble ourselves and He will heal the land.**

3. Worship means that you must build spiritual altars before God. **II Samuel 6:12-22, David twirled and danced before that Lord. "It was before the Lord that I danced."** It was an expression of Joy.

Principles for Building Worship
- True worshippers will cause God Almighty to come and dwell with them
- No matter what level we are on in God, we must continue to walk with God in our worship experience, in spirit and in truth
- As we walk with God as individuals our relationship with each other becomes more fertile and fruitful in Him, resulting in more freedom
- Continue to learn to offer praise and worship. Then submit your very life, your very will to Him as a living sacrifice of humble worship

The way to true worship is to seek the Kingdom of God, His righteous living and learn these three concepts in the process:

1. Get a clear <u>focus</u>
2. Walk in complete <u>fear</u> (reverence/worship)
3. And have a complete <u>faith</u> in Him

- God is waiting to do supernatural things for believers – But **He is also waiting for some risk-takers!** Risk-takers are worshippers that live on a high-level and high-intensity of worship. Why? Because these people have been developed through a lifestyle of worship through risk!
- Develop a lifestyle of worship to bring God into your environment, but it must be under His conditions and not your own. That's the developing process.
- II Samuel 24:14-19 – Because of David's sin to number the people, and because David was a worshipper, he took a **_risk_** that the Lord might kill him, but he went anyway to build an altar to the Lord on the threshing floor of Araunah the Jebsite.

Nothing To Lose

Now, as we worship, we move into a realm of what I call nothing to lose through the door of *Unlimited Possibilities.* I believe with all my heart that if you receive this word in your spirit, your way of doing things will change! I believe it will change ***TODAY, EVEN RIGHT NOW*** at this very moment!

Declare this with me: "I'm going to change because I'm going with God this day I have nothing to lose!"

How do you get to the place of *Unlimited Possibilities?* Worship!

God is saying…"Come on up into the Throne Room because this is where I will reveal Myself to you and share with you My desire for your life. My Son Jesus has given you access into My Throne Room. Come up, so I might reveal Myself to you in a new way and cause My Word to become real to you. If you will worship Me, you will know how to step forward and I will be with you to overthrow every enemy structure that is in your path*!* Ascend into My Throne Room as you worship, then descend into unlimited possibilities for your harvest. Let's go up!"

To ascend means to arise, to climb up, to come up - to get up, to grow up, to increase, to leap, to light up, to be raised up, to recover and to restore. This comes from the Hebrew word alah. We are to boldly rise up, ascend, go into the Throne Room and worship God! When we follow this sequence, God's strategies of restoration are revealed to us and the result is *Unlimited Possibilities.*

Acts 12:7 states, The angel told Peter…**"Arise quickly…"** Because there was an alah experience going on that Peter had to get to.

Even in the midst of death, when we alah, not even the surety of death can stop God from going into your prison, shining a light and bringing you out with His mighty Hand. I call that *Unlimited Possibilities* for the worshipper. The Bible goes on to say, (**I like this part**), "and his chains

fell off his hands." What chains are holding you down or holding you captive?

Because someone decided to alah, to ascend to worship, to go to heaven where God is, heaven decides to descend or release the resources and the strategies needed to free a man from chains. When you worship, this same God will send you the resources, the strategies you will need to fulfill your purpose in the earth through His *Unlimited Possibilities*.

Men, I challenge you to arise into a new place of freedom in worship!

Chapter Fourteen

CONCLUSION.....CURTAIN CALL

Revelation 19:7, "Let us be glad and rejoice, and give honor to him: For the marriage of the Lamb has come, and his wife has made herself ready." Scripture tells us that at the culmination of all human history, God will have a rejoicing bride. As Christ, as our Bridegroom, and the church as His bride, there will be dancing, celebration -- a heavenly wedding and then a feast!

In the words of one of my favorite songs..."When it's all been said and done, there is just one thing that matters. Did I do my best to live for truth -- did I live my life for you?" At the end of a Broadway musical, each performer comes to take a bow for the service they have just provided. I pray that one day I will hear "Well done thy good and faithful servant." The call to lead the nations in dance unto the Lord is an incredible privilege, one that will have eternal rewards.

Revelation 7:9-17, "After this I beheld, and, lo, a great multitude, which no man could number, of all nations, and kindreds, and people, and tongues, stood before the throne, and before the Lamb, clothed with white robes, and palms in their hands; And cried with a loud voice, saying, Salvation to our God which sitteth upon the throne, and unto the Lamb. And all the angels stood round about the throne, and about the elders and the four beasts, and fell before the throne on their faces, and worshipped God, saying, Amen: Blessing, and glory, and wisdom, and thanksgiving, and honour, and power, and might, be unto our God forever and ever. Amen. And one of the elders answered, saying unto me, What are these which are arrayed in white robes? and whence came they? And I said unto him, Sir, thou knowest. And he said to me, these are they which came out of great tribulation, and have washed their robes, and made them white in the blood of the Lamb. Therefore are they before the throne of God, and serve him day and night in his temple: and he that sitteth on the throne shall dwell among them. They shall hunger no more, neither thirst anymore; neither shall the sun light on them, nor any heat. For the Lamb which is in the midst of the throne shall feed them, and shall lead them unto living fountains of waters: and God shall wipe away all tears from their eyes."

Psalm 67 says, "God be merciful unto us, and bless us; and cause his face to shine upon us; Selah. That thy way may be known upon earth, thy saving health among all nations. Let the people praise thee, O God; let all the people praise thee. O let the nations be glad and sing for joy: for thou shalt judge the people righteously, and govern the nations upon earth. Selah. Let the people praise thee, O God; let all the people praise thee. Then shall the earth yield her increase; and God, even our own God, shall bless us. God shall bless us; and all the ends of the earth shall fear him.

Enroll Today!

The Eagles International Training Institute is a one year, in-depth training course for those who desire to soar to higher heights in the area of dance ministry. Our goal is to train and educate those called to the ministry of dance, and then release them to be effective servants, teachers, and leaders who will establish the Kingdom of God in all the earth. The Institute is very intense and requires a commitment to God's order, organization and Will for your life despite obstacles. Dr. Pamela Hardy is the Founder and Director of The Eagles International Training Institute and Set Free Evangelistic Ministries.

The Institute currently has over 300 graduates and over 100 Eagles currently enrolled from eighteen different countries! We have established schools in Puerto Rico and Holland.

EITI has 15 areas of training to equip you for the work of the ministry. We are soaring Eagles, going forth in the Spirit of the Lord God, anointed by His grace, called by His name, setting the captives free! We serve with a spirit of humility, we soar with the spirit of excellence!

For More Information on Dr. Pamela Hardy and/or EITI, please visit:
www.drpamelahardy.org or
www.eagleiti.org